Anger Management
for Everyone

Anger Management for Everyone

Seven Proven Ways to Control Anger and Live a Happier Life

RAYMOND CHIP TAFRATE, PH.D.
HOWARD KASSINOVE, PH.D., ABPP

 new**harbinger**publications, inc.

Library of Congress Cataloging-in-Publication Data

Tafrate, Raymond Chip.
   Anger management for everyone : seven proven ways to control anger and live a happier life / R. Chip Tafrate and Howard Kassinove.
      p. cm.
   Includes bibliographical references and index.
   ISBN 978-1-886230-83-5 (alk. paper)
1. Anger. 2. Conflict management. I. Kassinove, Howard. II. Title
   BF575.A5T35 2009
   152.4'7—dc22

                                                                2009017426

Publisher's Note

This publication is designed to provide accurate and authoritative information in regard to the subject matter covered. It is sold with the understanding that the publisher is not engaged in rendering psychological, legal, or other professional services. If expert assistance or counseling is needed, the services of a competent professional should be sought.

Cover design by Gayle Downs, Gayle Force Design, Atascadero, California
Composition by UB Communications, Parsippany, New Jersey
Printed in the United States of America on acid-free paper

Published by **Impact 🐢 Publishers®**

An Imprint of New Harbinger Publications, Inc.
             5674 Shattuck Avenue
             Oakland, CA 94609
             www.newharbinger.com

CONTENTS

PART 3: OTHER ISSUES

ACKNOWLEDGEMENTS

In 2002, we wrote *Anger Management: The Complete Treatment Guidebook for Practitioners*. We geared that text to professionals who were working with angry teenagers and adults. It was well received and was translated into Arabic, Korean, Russian, and Spanish. A lot of people sent us letters and emails telling us how useful the program in the book was. At the same time, we were aware that most people don't go to a professional for help with their anger issues. Thus, we decided to write *Anger Management for Everyone: Seven Proven Ways to Control Anger and Live a Happier Life* for people interested in learning on their own and helping themselves.

We certainly acknowledge the important work of our many colleagues. They have added to our understanding about anger, created skills for minimizing excessive reactions, and pioneered the development of positive life skills for happiness. However, since we wanted the book to read as smoothly as possible, citations that refer to scientific research aren't included in the chapters. Rather, references and suggestions for further reading are provided at the end of the book.

Some special people deserve recognition. First, we thank our many clients, patients, and students who have shared their personal anger experiences with us. Our knowledge and growth as professionals have improved as we've traveled with them through their personal stories and conflicts. Some colleagues who shaped our ideas and the entire field of anger management also deserve mention. These include Drs. Jerry Deffenbacher, Raymond DiGiuseppe, Albert Ellis, Raymond Novaco, and Joseph Wolpe. You will also notice that we have included clip art to highlight certain ideas and make the chapters more enjoyable. These images come from clipart.com and the copyright is held by JupiterImages.

We've been fortunate to have Impact Publishers' Dr. Robert Alberti, Melissa Froehner, and talented staff members guide us for many years to help us make our ideas more focused and user-friendly. We are also grateful for the support we received from our respective universities, Central Connecticut State University and Hofstra University, to study anger-related issues. Special thanks go to Dr. Gustavo Grodnitzky, Bruno Broll-Barone, and Anthony Iacovelli for their suggestions and feedback on the manuscript and Dr. Jeffrey Froh for encouraging us to think about the contributions of positive psychology to anger management. Finally, we greatly appreciate the support and love of our wives, Lauren Tafrate and Tina Kassinove, who have helped us live our own lives with minimal anger and maximum happiness.

— *Raymond Chip Tafrate and Howard Kassinove*

INTRODUCTION

What ticks you off? Is it your teenage son, who doesn't listen to your advice? How about your partner, who has a roving eye and sometimes doesn't come home when expected? Maybe your employer doesn't appreciate all the honest, hard work you do. Or perhaps your mother or father always seems to be picking on you. Parents can really drive you crazy, right?

And what about all those stupid drivers? They always seem to drive slowly in the fast lane, tailgate your car, or cut you off. They deserve to be shown a lesson! You can honk at them, glare them down, cut them off, and teach them to show you some respect. You can also yell at your children, mother, or husband. Or you can get really pissed off and tell your boss you're done! After all, those people had better learn you aren't going to take it anymore. At the very least, you might think it's important to show your anger and not let others bully you. And then there are the extremes:

> Frank was a thirty-six-year-old long-haul truck driver who was often out of town for up to two weeks at a time. Divorced from his first wife, he had been dating Amy for six months and thought they had agreed to stop seeing other people. Frank was even thinking about proposing to Amy. One day, after a five-day haul, he drove to Amy's house and saw a strange car in the driveway. Being naturally suspicious, he sneaked up to the bedroom window and looked inside. There he saw Amy having sex with another man.
>
> Frank became enraged. First he went to a local bar for a quick drink. Then he went to his apartment and got his shotgun. He went back to Amy's house and in his fit of anger killed both of them. The whole thing took less than an hour. Frank is now in prison for the rest of his life.

You're not Frank, of course, but how does anger show itself in your life? Since you're reading this book, you've probably thought a lot about that. Will life really be better if you keep on acting out of anger? Actually, as we'll show you in the upcoming chapters, anger is more likely to *make life worse.*

You might be thinking about your anger, or the anger of others, because you think it's time to do something about it. Or, a friend or a professional you're working with might have suggested this book to you. In any case, there's a good chance that your anger is something you can't ignore any longer. Your angry behavior might be scaring the people you loudly put down, make demands of, or threaten with gestures. Also, if you're looking honestly at yourself, you might be alarmed when you think about your own excessive reactions and where your anger is likely to lead you next.

We hope you aren't as enraged as Frank. Nevertheless, your anger might have reached a point where you, or a loved one, are concerned. Your anger probably doesn't just energize you to face problems; instead, it might be making it hard for you to think clearly and make good decisions. Your anger might not be improving your relationships and behaviors. Instead, it might be making people uncomfortable and ruining your closeness with others. In addition to helping you feel alive and passionate, your anger might lead you to impulsive and even aggressive and destructive acts. Indeed, you might be painfully aware of what anger is costing you.

As you learn to reduce your anger, you'll be able to make better decisions in your life, manage your relationships better, and behave in ways that are likely to bring about the results you want the most. Misfortune, unfairness, and disappointment are part of everyone's life; we'll show you how to think about such events — and respond to them — constructively.

This book is about putting anger in its proper place so you can live a vital, happy, and upbeat life. It's organized into three parts. The first part, chapters 1 to 3, contains information to help you understand anger and prepare to change. We'll answer some common questions about anger and ask you to become a keen observer of the details of your behavior when you are angry. We'll also ask you to look at your own arguments for — and against — changing your angry reactions.

In the second part, chapters 4 to 10, we present the seven skills that will help you bring your anger under control. These include changing how you relate to those situations that trigger your anger, learning to sidestep difficulties and come up with solutions to problems, learning to think differently about negative life events, and figuring out how to let go of anger at those who have mistreated you. We also cover skills that will help you to improve how you react when angry and to express yourself in a more effective, assertive way.

In the final part, chapters 11 and 12, we focus, first, on options to consider if your anger reactions continue to be a problem and, then, on how to use techniques from the field of positive psychology to live a more vibrant, joyful life.

Examples from our experiences with clients, patients, colleagues, and research participants will show you how to use the seven anger management skills in a lot of situations, including anger between friends and family members, in the workplace, at school, while parenting, in dating relationships, when driving, and when thinking about getting a divorce.

You can pick the elements of our program that are most likely to help you. At the same time, it's important to recognize that a self-help book can't be a substitute for a complete psychotherapy program if your anger remains a problem.

HOW TO GET THE MOST OUT OF THIS BOOK

- *Take your time.* This isn't the type of book to read through in one sitting. It's best to tackle one chapter at a time.

- *Be open.* Some information we present might go against ideas that you've had for years. Unfortunately, there's a lot of confusion about anger, and we hope you'll be open-minded about our recommendations.

- *Do the practice exercises.* Give them your best effort. Reading alone won't be enough for you to learn to control your anger.

- *Try to transfer the skills* discussed in the chapters to situations in your life. Repetition and lots of practice will make new ways of thinking and behaving more comfortable and automatic.

- *Feel free to move on* to the next skill if you try one and it doesn't fit well in that situation.

You probably noticed the word "proven" in our title. We would like to explain that. Our recommendations to you are based firmly on scientific findings and procedures from cognitive behavior therapy. Cognitive behavior therapy, or CBT, has produced the most advanced and scientifically supported techniques to help people improve their lives. In the world of science, however, very little is actually "proven." Rather, knowledge builds up over time as scientists learn more and more about behavior. Research and experience with helping people with anger issues show that the seven anger management techniques work.

The really good news is *you can learn to control your angry reactions*. And, you can experience greater happiness when you learn life-enriching lessons from positive psychology along with our anger reduction techniques.

PART I

ANGER BASICS

CHAPTER 1

ANGER 101: COMMON QUESTIONS AND ANSWERS

Never do anything when you are in a temper, for you will do everything wrong.

— BALTASAR GRACIAN, Spanish philosopher

We applaud you for examining the role that anger plays in your life. Anger can be really nasty. You might have firsthand experience with the pain and suffering that it produces. Anger can ruin relationships; it can increase the risk of heart attacks; and it's just plain unpleasant. At this point, you might not be sure that you can change the way you act when you're angry. We think you can! Reading this book is a big step toward living a more peaceful and productive life.

In this chapter, we'll help you make sense of the many parts of anger, and we'll answer common questions about it. Before we go there, however, we want to tell you the stories of Keith and Rebecca and Chuck. All three had difficulty managing their anger. Obviously, your life is different from theirs. We don't expect their stories to describe your issues and concerns. However, some of their struggles and problems are likely to be similar to yours.

The toxic effects of anger cut across many areas of life. So, throughout this book we present stories of people who have struggled with anger in a wide range of situations. Reacting strongly when angry is common. People of all ages, education levels, ethnic backgrounds, and income categories do it. What our examples have in common is that *anger got in the way* of dealing effectively with life challenges. At some point, you'll have to ask yourself this basic question: Is your anger really helpful?

Keith and Rebecca: Marital Discord

Keith and Rebecca had a rocky marriage right from the start. They bickered constantly about little things, such as who was to take care of the laundry and who would decide which TV channel to watch. Every time, each accused the other of being unfair, being uncooperative, and causing the argument. When Rebecca became pregnant in the second year of their marriage, they both thought that the joy of being new parents would bring them closer together. Unfortunately, the opposite was true. The stress and hard work of parenting made their differences worse, increased their blaming, and multiplied their destructive arguments. Eventually, they both concluded that divorce was the only option since neither one was willing to change. Of course, through the divorce process, they couldn't agree on money, a custody arrangement for their daughter, or how to split up furniture and other things. They both hired a lawyer to fight for the best possible divorce agreement. They fought bitterly over every issue and didn't give an inch.

More than a year of legal wrangling left both of them with high debts because of the lawyers' fees. In addition, they each found the final agreement to be blatantly unfair. Although they shared the responsibility and custody of their daughter, their anger continued and showed itself in a variety of ways. Keith was uncooperative, said nasty things to their daughter about Rebecca, and was inconsistent in his child support payments. Rebecca wouldn't let their daughter talk to Keith on the telephone and wouldn't stick to the visitation schedule, often "forgetting" to drop their daughter off for visits. Neither could rise above his or her own anger to see the bad effects their disagreements were having on their daughter, who was rapidly becoming shy and anxious.

You can probably remember plenty of times when your anger seemed justified — almost proper. If you're like most people, you've probably said to yourself, "I have a *right* to be angry after what he or she did!" Yet, if you're honest with yourself, you can recognize that there have been other times when your anger was too strong, lasted too long, created unnecessary problems, or was just plain foolish. You can probably recall times your anger led to arguments, headaches, regrets, stupid behaviors,

Chuck: The Angry Father

Chuck was a forty-two-year-old father who, in fits of temper, argued with his seventeen-year-old teenage son, Kwami, almost every day. They quarreled about Kwami's friends, clothes, music, homework, lack of motivation, attitude toward authority, and desire to get tattoos and piercings. Although some of Chuck's concerns were realistic, his methods to fix the problems weren't working and his anger was making the situation worse. In addition to frequent screaming in an effort to make his son "improve," Chuck became so upset that he "had to" have two or three drinks every night "just to calm down." As a result, his relationship with his wife became tense, and his sleep patterns became erratic. Chuck often fell asleep early, only to wake up at 2:00 or 3:00 AM and obsess about how to make Kwami recognize the error of his ways.

A salesperson, Chuck initially saw himself as "normal" and "loving" and told us that everyone he knew became angry and argued almost every day — especially with teenage kids. His belief that "I'm normal" and "My son's the problem," meant that Chuck wasn't yet ready to see the problem with his anger. Chuck didn't understand the negative effect that his yelling and bickering was having on the self-image and achievement of his son and his other children. He also didn't realize that the daily anger-fueled arguments, drinking, and sleep problems were affecting his marriage, his productivity at work, and his health. His employer eventually put him on probation because of poor job performance.

and other problems. Anger can be difficult to understand. In fact, you might have felt both happy *and* unhappy after you expressed anger. You might have believed that your anger was appropriate, at the same time realizing that it accomplished nothing and led only to more problems.

Anger is one of our basic feelings. Scholars — including naturalist Charles Darwin, evolutionary psychologist Dr. Robert Plutchik, and University of California professor emeritus of psychology Dr. Paul Ekman — have told us that anger is found in people in all cultures and from all parts of the world. Anger is common in families, workplaces, and most relationships. Anger, like other emotions, is woven into the fabric of human existence.

Some aspects of anger are positive. It's part of the ups and downs of relationships and can be a useful signal that something isn't right. *Some* anger can even improve understanding between people. A raised, angry voice can tell others you're talking about something important, leading them to listen more carefully to you. Anger might motivate you to make changes in your life or even face problems that you've been avoiding. Anger can also lead to zest, excitement, and passion. The plain truth is that we wouldn't want to live in a world without feelings such as anger. Anger does have some benefits; so this book isn't about eliminating anger entirely from your life.

On the other hand, anger can lead to significant loss and suffering. Damage to relationships with family members, friends, and co-workers is a common consequence of anger. Angry people "think crookedly" and make bad decisions. Long-term anger goes along with severe medical problems, such as heart disease and stroke. These are just a few reasons to keep your anger under control. We'll give you some other reasons as you read on.

UNDERSTANDING ANGER

"Why do I get angry?" "Why do others in my life treat me so rotten?" "How can I make my life better?"

As psychologists, we've worked with a lot of adults and teenagers over the years and noticed that the same questions come up over and over again. Our goal in this chapter is to answer some basic questions about anger, provide you with accurate information, and build a base of knowledge you can draw on as you move forward to improve your behavior when you're angry.

What Is Anger?

Anger is something that happens inside your body. It's an emotional response you consciously feel. At its core, anger is an internal awareness of specific thoughts, feelings, and desires. Let's take a closer look at its elements.

Self-talk. The first element of anger is self-talk. These are the words you say to yourself that you don't usually share with others. This is perfectly normal. We think in words and we all have a steady stream of dialogue going on inside our heads all day long. When you're angry, you might be saying something to yourself like, "How could that bitch do that to me? I hate her," "He's a real jerk. I'd like to really make him suffer," "That's so unfair," or "I'm really pissed off!"

A father might think, "I can't take those kids anymore. Their behavior is intolerable. They never listen. I'm just infuriated with them. I've gotta get out of here." Or a businesswoman might say to herself, "I'm really angry. My co-workers just don't appreciate what I do for them and how I cover for their errors. I'll show them. I'm not going to fix things anymore, and we'll see what the boss says then!"

Angry self-talk has common elements, including:

- a description of the feeling ("I feel annoyed/angry/furious.")

- an exaggerated description of the problem ("This situation is just terrible.")

- blame ("My boss made me so angry. It's his fault.")

- a belief in your inability to cope with problems ("I just can't deal with it anymore. I can't take her laziness.")

- morally based thoughts ("She should have acted properly. Good people don't do things like that.")

- a condemning idea ("She's a total jerk, a real piece of scum.")

- thoughts about revenge ("I'll show her who the real boss is!")

Self-talk is sometimes shared with others. If the angry person is dominant and feels justified, as when a parent argues with a child, these internal thoughts might be screamed out loud. At work, however, negative thoughts about a supervisor might be held in due to fear of being fired or being passed over for a promotion. Likewise, at school, students often hold in their angry thoughts about teachers out of fear of being given a bad grade. In these instances, the anger is likely to be expressed indirectly by gossiping with others rather than dealing directly with the problem.

Images. People often recall images of the event that led to their anger. In your head you might see your boss giving you a reprimand. You might catch your teenager swearing in a disagreement with his brother and then storming out to be with his friends. You might see your wife or girlfriend flirting with another person while ignoring you. These images might occur during the daytime hours as you privately dwell on the problem or talk about it with a friend; however, they might be most vivid when you're alone, especially when you're about to fall asleep. You might also have images and fantasies about revenge or getting even. For example, you might see yourself telling someone off, winning an argument, or even shoving someone. The danger, of course, is that such images can fuel actual aggressive behavior.

Sensations in your body. When you're angry, you might become aware of sensations in your body such as a knotted stomach, tight shoulders, sweating, or a headache. Although you might not notice any physical symptoms until later, you might sense your own tight fist or pursed lips at the moment of anger. In this sense, anger is an "excitement" emotion. You can feel your body becoming energized to take some form of action, such as shouting, breaking something, or resisting the ideas of others.

Patterns of expression. Figure out if you're generally an "innie" or an "outie" when it comes to expressing your anger. Your anger might be something you usually keep to yourself. You might believe that you'll suffer negative consequences if you're honest or yell and let others know how you feel. Over the years, you might have learned to always keep a lid on your anger and to never express it. You might be like that old-fashioned kitchen pressure cooker, which had a tight seal so that no steam could get out. You're an "innie" if you generally boil inside but seem cool on the outside. Jake's story on the next page shows this type of pattern.

Some people show their anger by yelling, screaming, arguing, and being sarcastic. This can escalate to slamming books, breaking things, and shoving people. If this is you, you're an "outie." You might be aware of the potential negative results of such behavior, but you let others have it anyway. "Outies" sometimes say, "I just don't care what happens. I can't take it anymore. I've just gotta express what I feel."

Being an "outie" can lead you to have significant problems with others, as few of us like to be near people who are so outwardly angry. Paul, a twenty-six-year-old graduate student, told us that he was afraid of his father for all of his childhood. His father yelled at and belittled him almost daily, so Paul avoided him. Paul was surprised to learn that most

Jake: Holding It All In

Jake was a forty-four-year-old assistant principal in an inner city high school. He was well trained, with a Ph.D. in administration, and he considered himself a good educator. Unfortunately, Jake, who was white, was constantly concerned that he would lose his job to a minority educator. This concern led him to be overly cautious with his peers and superiors. Jake never expressed annoyance, disappointment, or anger. On the surface, he agreed with everyone, no matter what they said. If he disagreed, Jake kept quiet. He never took sides. Internally, however, Jake spent hours in his office or at home stewing about what he saw as the unfairness and shortcomings of the system. He suffered from frequent headaches and stomach upset and often had difficulty sleeping. Although he was generally well liked, he never expressed his ideas for educational change in a forceful manner. As a consequence, Jake was never promoted to school principal.

of the other students were *not* afraid of their fathers. Another example of this style of expression is described in Andy's story on the next page.

Some people are neither an "innie" nor an "outie"; they routinely hold their anger in, but at times of great frustration they let it out. Perhaps you're like this. If this is how you act, it's important to figure out when you're most likely to squelch your anger and when you're likely to let it out.

Anger consists of the following elements:

- self-talk
- images
- sensations in your body
- patterns of expression

In chapter 2, we'll return to these elements and assist you in analyzing your own anger patterns.

What Causes Anger?

In truth, there are a lot of different causes of anger. That's why you see experts expressing many different opinions in the newspapers, on radio,

Andy: Business and Medical Problems

Andy started an accounting firm with his old friend Rob. For five years, the business prospered and profits rose. However, things eventually began to level off, and although new clients were calling for services the company's net income dropped significantly. This led to discussions, and eventually to big arguments about how many employees to hire and how much time Andy and Rob were devoting to the business, and finally to a break in their friendship. The arguments became more intense, with each partner accusing the other of not working hard enough and not living up to his end of the business agreement.

In frustration, Andy decided to spend a quiet weekend at the office to look over the books. He discovered that Rob had been paying a lot to an advertising agency to get more business. He also thought that Rob was paying their employees too much and allowing them to take off too much time with pay. Furious, he confronted Rob, and they had a major argument. Andy shouted, slammed books against the office table, and made vague threats about "what's going to happen." Throughout the argument, Rob denied any wrongdoing and tried to explain his actions to Andy. Andy, however, turned a deaf ear to Rob's explanation. Both men began to devote less time to the business, and income continued to decrease. Eventually, they dissolved the company. Unfortunately, Andy had no savings to open a new business. After being out of work for three months, he got a lower paying job at a local payroll company. He became depressed and developed heart problems that required expensive daily medications.

and on TV. Let's begin with the answer that pulls together what is accepted by most professionals who study and treat anger:

> Anger is an emotional reaction to the unwanted and often unexpected behavior of others. It develops when you sense a threat to your physical well-being, property, personal image, sense of fairness, or reasonable desire for comfort. How you communicate anger depends on where you are and on whether expressing anger has worked for you in the past.

This rather formal answer refers first to what we call an "immediate cause." Something bad happens (like learning that a friend has been gossiping about you), and you immediately respond with anger. You blame the other person for the way *you* act when you're angry. Psychologists call this a "stimulus to response" pattern. The stimulus is the friend who was gossiping about you; the response is your anger. It turns out that this explanation is both too simple and wrong. As you'll see in chapter 3, we call this "the big mistake." Here are some other explanations about the causes of anger.

Learning. The truth is that a lot of your anger comes from habits that you've developed over years. Although there's always some immediate trigger that gets you going, you've been learning *when* and *how* to become angry for a long time.

Learning often involves what psychologists call "modeling." This means learning by seeing what happens to other people when they get angry (in other words, learning by example). People tend to copy the actions of others, especially when they believe that those actions produce good results. Learning by modeling can come from watching the angry behaviors of parents, peers, or characters on TV, in movies, in sermons, and in video games, to name just a few examples. There are a lot of opportunities to learn about anger this way. Then you take what you've learned about anger and turn it into rules for yourself, such as, "If people disrespect or gossip about me, *I'll* get furious and yell. That's *me* and that's what *I* do!"

Not all angry behavior comes from observing others. You have your own unique, personal experiences and learning history. Your learning history is made up of two parts; psychologists call these two parts "reinforcement" and "punishment." Although you probably don't think much about it, all your behaviors are followed by consequences. You tend to repeat behaviors that result in consequences you like. So, if you angrily yell at your son to clean his room and he does it, you're more likely to yell at him again in the future. Behaviors that are "reinforced" in the short-term become long-term habits.

"Punishment," on the other hand, occurs when your behaviors are followed by something you don't like. For example, if you angrily tell some strangers in a movie theater to be quiet and they respond by cursing at you, which in turn results in a noisy and uncomfortable confrontation, you're less likely to tell strangers to be quiet in the future. Behaviors that are "punished" in the short-term don't become habits.

Over time, "reinforcements" and "punishments" shape your habits powerfully. The way you act now when you're angry has a lot to do with the consequences of your past angry behaviors.

Thinking. Certain ways of thinking also cause anger. For example, you might misinterpret or distort what other people do or say; you might exaggerate, making small problems into "big deals"; or you might be demanding and inflexible in your views. When angry, you probably believe that:

- you've been neglected, ignored, or treated unfairly;
- someone else has acted wrongly;
- the person who angered you could have acted better if he or she really wanted to;
- the person who angered you should have acted better.

Your beliefs about the behavior of others may or may not be true. There might be times when you've been mistaken about the motives of other people. Maybe the friend who isn't returning your calls or responding to your emails is dealing with personal health problems or those of a family member. The potential date who keeps putting you off might be overwhelmed with work projects. Or maybe your teen daughter, who is supposed to come home by dinnertime, was late because she stopped at the mall to buy you a birthday present; she wouldn't want to tell you that and spoil the surprise.

If you're like most people, you don't evaluate your thinking about bad treatment at the hands of others. Your thoughts just seem to come automatically. Unfortunately, over time your conclusions can become distorted, inaccurate, and exaggerated. In that sense, it's your *thinking* that causes your anger. We'll return to this idea in chapter 6 and show you how to evaluate and change the parts of your thinking that are exaggerated and distorted.

Human nature. Finally, it turns out that anger is part of human nature. The reasons for angry and aggressive behaviors in other animals are similar to ours. Monkeys, for example, show anger when their territory is invaded and when other monkeys try to steal their food or mate with their partners. Other animals do things when they're angry to make themselves look big and strong. These include making their bodies look bigger, standing on their hind legs, hissing, growling, biting, kicking, and scratching. These behaviors are like a lot of our own. When animals growl or hiss, it's a signal to keep away. Our shouting is like their growling.

When animals stand erect and enlarge themselves, they're saying that they're too powerful to mess with. That's similar to our waving a fist or leaning forward in a threatening pose. Anger comes out when you feel threatened because it worked for prehistoric humans. At the same time, we point out that our similarity to other animals leads only to a *tendency* to act with anger. As humans who are also shaped by thinking, "reinforcement," families, schools, and churches, we do have the power to overcome such tendencies.

What Is Aggression?

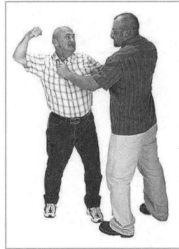

Anger and its cousin aggression are often confused. Anger is an *emotion* you feel inside. Aggression is a *behavior* others can observe. Aggressive behaviors include throwing and banging things as well as kicking, shoving, hitting, and bullying. It also includes sneaky, indirect actions, such as scratching someone's car or hiding office supplies from a co-worker you dislike.

Aggressive behaviors range from minor — a teen throwing an eraser at a school friend in annoyance — to serious — assault and murder. When we say that some aggression is minor, we don't mean to say it isn't serious. We believe all intentionally destructive behavior directed against us or another person is unacceptable. Nonetheless, different aggressive acts will have different negative consequences. Being hit by an eraser in school is minor in comparison to being pushed down the stairs. As shown in the story of Roscoe, acting aggressively when angry can lead to problems with the law.

Finally, there's the issue of intent. For something that your husband, wife, child, or co-worker did to be considered aggressive, it had to have

Roscoe: Anger and the Law

Roscoe was a twenty-two-year-old single man who lived in a rough urban area. He grew up poor, didn't finish high school, and served several short prison terms for disorderly conduct and brawling. Roscoe was unsuccessful in his attempts to find steady construction work. As hard as he tried, most jobs usually ended badly because of disagreements with his supervisors or co-workers. On several occasions, the verbal quarrels escalated into threatening, yelling, and shoving. Roscoe believed that he had to deal with more than his fair share of misfortunes and bad treatment from co-workers over the years. So, he said he doesn't "take any crap from anyone." In addition, most of his dating relationships lasted less than a few months and he didn't have many close friends.

In spite of his lack of career or social success, Roscoe rarely admitted to feeling sad or worried. He said that such emotions are wimpy and would make him look vulnerable. But anger was different. Roscoe said his anger made him feel strong and in control, especially when people didn't treat him the way he liked. Out of work and money, Roscoe decided to break into a local home. He was caught and was given a four-year prison term. While in prison, he had an argument with an inmate who made a nasty remark about Roscoe's receding hairline. Roscoe immediately became infuriated and hit the man with a chair. As a result, he was sentenced to an additional three years in prison.

been done intentionally. We don't usually consider dentists or physical therapists to be aggressive, even though they might cause some temporary pain. Their intent is to help us. The law looks at intentional and unintentional crimes as very different. Intentional aggression, as when a murder is planned, is punished much more severely than is unintentional aggression, as when a person is hurt in a car accident. A friend's intentional bad behavior is far more significant than accidental behavior. When examining the bad behaviors of others in your life, you'd be wise to consider whether their actions were intentional or not.

Does Anger Cause Aggression?

Sometimes anger is the fuel for aggression. More often, however, anger occurs without aggression. And, sometimes aggressive acts occur without anger. Hunters, for example, are aggressive; their intent is to kill the animals. Yet, they don't harbor anger against those animals. If you look at stories reported in the newspapers, it would seem as though anger and aggression are like conjoined twins. You often read about crimes of passion in which an enraged man attacks his girlfriend after an argument, an angry employee assaults a supervisor after she isn't given a raise, or an angry teenager shoots his teachers or classmates after he's rejected or misunderstood.

These high-profile cases distort the picture of the relationship between anger and aggression. A lot of the aggression we see on the news and hear about *is* connected to anger. This makes it look like anger and aggression *always* occur together. But this is actually the exception, not the rule.

The truth is that intentional physical aggression follows anger only about 10 percent of the time. Most of the time anger occurs alone, and it's the anger alone that's the real problem for most people. Ninety percent of the time anger shows itself only as yelling, arguing, frowning, getting in a bad mood, or pouting — not as aggression. Even when someone threatens another (for example, the irate parent who says, "I'm really gonna let you have it!"), aggression typically doesn't follow anger.

Nevertheless, anger sometimes *is* followed by aggression. Whether or not it does, anger is a serious problem in its own right.

Aggression and harm to other humans can occur without anger. For example, a New York teenager thoughtlessly threw a frozen turkey from an overpass onto a passing car, and a driver was severely hurt. Yet the teen wasn't angry with the driver. In fact, he had no idea who his thoughtless action might hurt. Other examples include times when teenagers and adults have behaved aggressively, not out of anger but as part of a plan to steal from others. When interrupted during the theft, they might have hurt whoever happened to be around. The perpetrators weren't angry with their victims; their goal was simply to steal something.

Again, we don't want to downplay the importance of the relationship between anger and aggression. When anger leads to arousal and physical excitement along with thoughts about revenge, it can lead to aggressive behavior. Some people have strong connections between their anger and aggression. They think being angry makes it OK to be aggressive. In chapter 2, when we examine the anger episode model, you'll be asked to carefully examine your own anger patterns and the connection between your internal anger experiences and your outward aggressive behaviors.

Is My Anger Normal?

You might wonder if your own pattern of anger is normal. One way to answer this question is to consider whether situations in your life typically improve or get worse after you become angry.

Another way to answer this question is to consider the frequency, intensity, and duration of your anger. *How often* do you become angry? Our research shows that about one quarter of adults become angry one or more times each week. Some people get angry almost every day. Becoming angry seems to often go along with a variety of problems such as headaches, a bad self-image, depression, guilt, weaker relationships with friends and family members, and medical and legal troubles. Another 25 percent of adults seem to rarely, if ever, become angry. These people seem to live much happier lives, with far fewer personal, medical, and legal problems.

How strong is your anger? The anger we're calling normal involves a moderate intensity of feeling. The notion of moderation is further discussed in chapter 2. Obviously, the more intense your anger is, the more likely it is to cause problems for you. Mild annoyance doesn't create serious disruptions in the lives of most people.

How long does your anger last? For some people, anger continues over long periods of time. Days, weeks, or months can be spent dwelling on past unfairness and crappy treatment at the hands of others. Remaining angry for long periods interferes with moving on with life and experiencing joy and happiness.

Think about some of the times you've been angry. Have you considered whether your anger was too weak, just right, or too strong? Does your anger occur too often? Does it last too long? Although anger can *sometimes* be a good thing, you have to look carefully at your life and decide if it's helping or hurting you.

Do Men Get Angrier Than Women?

Another common question has to do with differences between men and women. Most people believe that men are more angry and explosive than women. The reality is that men and women are much more alike than they are different, and a lot of scientists have even found that women become angry more often than men. For example, a large-scale review of scientific studies was published in 2000 by psychologist Dr. John Archer from the University of Central Lancashire. He concluded that women were slightly more likely than men to become angry and to use physical aggression. Of course, since men generally are stronger, when they aggress against women they produce more harm.

Another large study was published in 1997 by psychologist Dr. Lynn Magdol and colleagues at the University of Wisconsin. They concluded that "Physical violence perpetration (toward others) was reported by 37.2% of women and 21.8% of men." Their findings are about both anger and aggression, and also show that slightly more women than men report angry behaviors.

In our professional experience there's a lot of anger in both men and women. Both sexes seem to become angry for the same reasons, feel anger the same way, and express themselves in similar ways. So if you're a woman or a man who is reading this book, you're definitely not alone. And, keep in mind that the skills and techniques that we present in the following chapters work equally well for both genders.

Let Anger Out or Hold Anger In?

People often ask us if it's better to hold anger in or let it out. That's the wrong question; both are bad. It's unwise to hold anger in for long periods of time, and it's unwise to express it impulsively and strongly. Rather, the goal is to minimize anger and to express it thoughtfully in a way that's likely to lead to problem resolution. That's what we want to teach in this book. Our program will teach you how to minimize the flames of your anger. You'll learn how to express your anger assertively and how to seek constructive dialogue to reduce arguments with others. For those times when it's impossible to express your anger and seek dialogue, we'll teach you how to relax, forgive, lower the anger flame, and move forward with life.

Does Anger Make Other Problems Worse?

Yes, excessive anger leads to a range of emotional, behavioral, and medical problems. The most common are anxiety, depression, the abuse of substances such as alcohol and drugs, and heart disease.

You've probably noticed you're more likely to become angry when you're worried about important life events such as problems at work or school or with the behavior of your children, family members, or friends. As your anxiety rises, your anger fuse becomes shorter. You become less able to tolerate minor frustrations or unwanted hassles. You're clearly more vulnerable to becoming angry when you're anxious or feel threatened. Similarly, the negative outcomes that result from your anger often make difficult situations worse. Reacting with anger seldom solves problems and often creates more. So, anger and anxiety can be part of a vicious cycle.

The same is true for the relationship between anger and sadness. You might have noticed that you're also more prone to angry reactions when you're feeling blue and "down in the dumps." Some people go back and forth between feeling sad and hopeless and reacting angrily to life's challenges. Furthermore, acting in anger can lead to losses, failures, and isolation. Not being able to negotiate the problems of life can very well set the stage for depression.

Anger sometimes goes along with substance abuse. You might be tempted to take tranquilizers or sleeping pills or drink alcohol to try to relax or calm the tense physical symptoms of anger. These methods are habit forming, and dependency can come quickly. Some folks, unfortunately, resort to street drugs to cope with their anger, which leads to even more problems.

If you suffer with any of these issues, we think our seven proven ways to control anger will help you. Often, the techniques can also be used to reduce anxiety and depression. Chapter 11 provides recommendations for working to reduce your anger and deal effectively with other issues at the same time.

There's another set of concerns connected with anger that usually is overlooked. As we told you earlier, it turns out that intense and prolonged anger goes along with a number of serious medical conditions such as heart disease, stroke, high blood pressure, and perhaps even diabetes. Over time, strong anger experiences are likely to take a toll on your physical health. These types of medical conditions usually don't emerge right away but rather appear after years of anger-related difficulties. Getting a handle on the way you act when you're angry might be more important than you first realized.

CHANGING THE WAY YOU ACT WHEN YOU'RE ANGRY

Changing your behavior and learning to manage your emotions, such as anger, can be hard. It takes thoughtful analysis and practice to change, whether we're talking about quitting smoking or drinking, changing spending habits, or improving relationships. As for anger expression, there are some short-term good results: momentary self-righteousness, a sense of power, a feeling of control, or the impression that others listen to your demands or stop criticizing you. You might even savor thoughts of revenge.

Such immediate satisfactions keep anger going. Coupled with our natural tendency to react when threatened, these forces make change difficult. Nevertheless, the seven proven techniques you'll learn in this book are powerful, and we're confident that with practice you can improve the way you act when you're angry and change for the better.

In terms of moving forward, the next step is to understand exactly what happens when you get angry. Breaking your individual anger episodes down into manageable pieces is the topic of the next chapter. Then in later chapters, we'll help you develop the seven proven skills that lead to better anger control.

KEY POINTS TO REMEMBER

- Anger is an emotion — something you feel inside your body — that can energize you to take constructive or destructive action.

- Aggression is different from anger. Aggression refers to behaviors such as hitting, bullying, shoving, and destroying property.

- Anger doesn't automatically lead to aggression.

- Anger comes from learning (habits), ways of thinking, and your human nature.

- To figure out if your anger is normal, think about whether your problems get better or worse after you become angry.

- Men and women become angry for the same reasons, and feel and express anger in similar ways.

- Your anger is probably self-defeating if it's frequent, intense, or long lasting.

- Anger is related to anxiety, depression, alcohol and drug use, heart disease, and stroke.

- Ask yourself the following question: "Is my anger helping or hurting me?" Be honest!

CHAPTER 2

UNDERSTANDING ANGER EPISODES

Anger: an acid that can do more harm to the vessel in which it is stored than to anything on which it is poured.

— SENECA, Roman philosopher

Your anger probably seems to explode without a warning. The truth is that anger occurs as part of a chain of events. All anger episodes follow a predictable pattern. Examining and understanding your pattern is the first step toward achieving better control. We call this examination an "anger episode analysis." It will be helpful to look at your reactions from this perspective.

Most people believe that the crummy behavior of others or some other external event is responsible for their anger. In the next chapter, we refer to this as the "big mistake." In reality, a combination of external events and how you evaluate or interpret those events causes anger. In other words, how you think about a difficulty or a challenge in your life has a lot to do with the extent of your anger.

Chances are also good that you've developed patterns of how you experience and express anger. These might include thoughts you have or images you see in your head, physical sensations in your body, and physical reactions such as yelling, tightening up, or sulking. In this chapter, we help you see these patterns more clearly. By understanding the unique features of your anger experiences, it will be much easier to make changes in what have previously seemed to be automatic reactions. In addition, understanding the components of your anger episodes will help you examine the results and clearly see when anger is working for

Harvey: The Furious Boss

Harvey, aged thirty-nine, managed a building products business that his father had begun fifty years earlier. With great pride, they sold roofing, siding, and other home products both to the public and to professional contractors. The products were priced at a 20 percent discount for the contractors, who then installed them in homes. Homeowners paid the retail price. Harvey saw himself as a caring boss, and he oversaw a sales force of twenty people and thirty workers in the warehouse. The business was very successful, and there was plenty of money in the bank account. Harvey lived well, as did his senior employees. When things went well on the sales floor, Harvey was very pleasant to be around.

However, when someone made a mistake, an uglier side of him emerged. The most common mistakes were about the issues of pricing and delivery dates. On occasion, a salesperson would wrongly sell to a retail customer at the wholesale price. Also, a promise was sometimes made to deliver goods that weren't in stock. When Harvey discovered such an error, he would immediately erupt with anger. In front of the other employees and customers, Harvey would scream at the salesperson: "How could you be so stupid? I don't understand how you could do this. Didn't you check stock in the warehouse? You've been with us for five years and should know better. You've really made a mess. Damn!" Harvey did this to almost every employee. He never threatened to fire people or demote them; he just exploded in anger about the mistake and then went to his office. It usually took more than an hour for him to cool down. When we spoke to Harvey, he said he had been like that all of his life. He said, "My anger just erupts. I don't understand what happens. It's beyond me." Harvey had no idea about the stages he went through when he became angry. Becoming more aware of these was his first step toward achieving better control.

you and when it isn't. Reading about Harvey will show you how people can become confused about how their own anger reactions emerge.

Because the Anger Episode Analysis Model is simple and increases self-awareness, it will provide you with a sense of mastery over your anger. Then, as you move into part 2 of this book, you can spend more time on the skills you think will be on target — and helpful — for your particular patterns.

ANGER EPISODE ANALYSIS

We developed the Anger Episode Analysis Model based on our studies about how people experience anger in the real world. Our studies included people from across the United States and from other countries, including Russia and India. The model consists of five parts: anger triggers, evaluations, personal experiences, expressive patterns, and outcomes.

The best way for you to understand your anger is to apply this analysis to one of your own anger experiences. We would like you to think of a recent example in which you felt strong anger. As you go through this

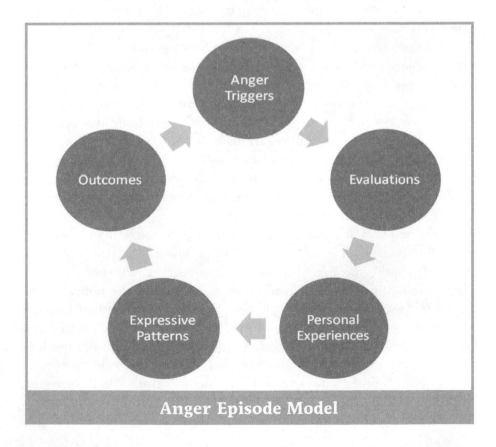

Anger Episode Model

chapter, you'll be asked questions about different aspects of this anger event. Write your responses in the boxes provided throughout sections of this chapter. Be sure to use the same example for the entire chapter. Your goal is to thoroughly examine all the components of this single anger episode.

Triggers

The anger sequence starts with a triggering event. Triggers are usually everyday situations that involve a challenge to your ideas or behavior, a disagreement, a struggle about what to do, or a disappointment. Many times, some kind of stress, threat, unfairness, loss, or potential loss is involved. Let's review some of the most common triggers.

Negative behaviors of others. By far, the most commonly reported anger triggers are unwanted — and sometimes unexpected — actions (or inactions) of other people. These include being ignored, disrespected, or rejected, as when your ideas are criticized or dismissed or your hard work is taken for granted. We've heard a lot of people say, "He doesn't even listen to my ideas," "She just wants to do what she wants," "He didn't support my sales plan," or "After I spent three hours looking for her gift, she said I wasn't thoughtful." Interestingly, we've found that most often, people tend to get angry with others in their lives who they love or like. Although we all occasionally become angry at strangers, if you review your own anger patterns, you'll likely see that most of your anger occurs when you deal with people you're close to, such as children, parents, husbands or wives, live-in boyfriends or girlfriends, co-workers, and friends.

Sometimes an action that most people would judge to be good can become an anger trigger. Consider Maria, an account executive at a major firm who was told every day by a co-worker that she was "hot." After the first few so-called compliments, she found the remark to be very offensive and she eventually became angry. Or consider Liora, a new mother who received a constant stream of unsolicited advice from her mother-in-law about how to raise her child. Although her mother-in-law had good intentions and her advice was often solid, over time Liora experienced the advice as irritating and it led to anger, quarrelling, and avoiding her mother-in-law. Unwanted behavior, whether it's a good thing or a bad thing, can become a trigger for anger.

Inanimate objects. Perhaps you've gotten angry with a computer, MP3 player, DVD player, cell phone, car, or copy machine when it stopped working properly. People sometimes scream at, throw, or punch the thing they're mad at. For some people, destroying expensive property in fits of anger becomes a real problem. In one story of self-defeat, thirty-four-year-old Jessica became angry at a public washing machine in the basement of her apartment building. The machine took only one-dollar bills and all she had was a five-dollar bill. In a fit of anger, she broke the door on the machine, an act that was recorded by the security camera. Her anger cost her five hundred dollars. Most people, of course, feel foolish after they've expressed anger at objects.

Anger at your own behavior. You might experience anger in relation to your *own* actions. In other words, you might be angry with yourself about something you've done and regretted. Lara, a thirty-two-year-old cashier, said to us, "I'm so angry at myself for letting him do that to me." And Phyllis, a twenty-seven-year-old homemaker, said, "I'm pissed at myself for not saying something to her." If self-directed anger is a trigger for you, it's likely you experience additional emotions when you're angry such as guilt, shame, and sadness.

Extreme circumstances. Some anger develops from traumatic events such as physical or sexual assault, being robbed, the unexpected death of a loved one, a natural disaster such as a hurricane or a fire, or a crippling illness. Although life is unpredictable and everyone is vulnerable to such experiences, extreme life events can lead to long-term, enduring anger with fantasies of revenge. As we discuss in chapter 7, remaining angry isn't the only option for dealing with extreme circumstances. Indeed, bitterness doesn't contribute to mental health.

Memories about the past. Anger can be triggered when you think about having been abused or treated unfairly. Thoughts of this mistreatment can take on a life of their own and become obsessive. These memories can be about the recent or distant past — including childhood — and range from relatively minor mistreatment (as when twenty-four-year-old Ken said to us, "I know that my mother loved me, but she seemed to pay more attention to my learning disabled brother.") to more extreme life-altering circumstances (such as physical abuse).

There's one more important point about anger triggers. Generally we all become angry about the same kinds of relationships or events.

So even if you struggle with anger, it's likely that you're reacting to the same situations that we all experience from time to time. However, your reactions might be more extreme and will then lead to worse results. Knowledge about the triggering events of your anger is important because it helps you identify the typical starting points that disrupt your life.

To sum it all up, a wide variety of actions by others and situations can set the stage for anger. However, the most common anger trigger is an unwanted, unexpected, negative action by another person who is well known and liked or loved.

Now, we'd like you to think about one of your own recent anger experiences and how it began. In the Trigger box, identify specific aspects of the trigger. Although you can simply *think* about the anger trigger, it might be more useful if you write down your answers. Analyzing an anger episode begins by being specific about the situation that started the event.

Evaluations

Human beings are thinking creatures. We constantly evaluate what's going on in front of us. We also think and plan for the future and reflect

---

Trigger

Describe the event that led to your anger:

_____

_____

Approximate date and time of your anger episode: _____

_____

The place where it occurred: ___ at home ___ at work ___ at school ___ other (describe): _____

The target (persons or object) of my anger was: _____

The situation surrounding my anger was: _____

_____

---

on events that have already happened. Knowledge about thinking is necessary to understand anger.

To understand the role of our evaluations (thoughts, judgments, and appraisals) in the chain of events that lead to anger, consider the example of teasing. People tease each other to strengthen relationships, to flirt, to pass time and play with each other, and to resolve conflicts and bad feelings. Although a lot of teasing is done in fun, it can lead to anger, shame, or humiliation if it's viewed as insulting rather than playful. Saying something playfully like "Well, aren't you a know-it-all," can lead to laughter — or anger — depending on how it's interpreted.

We once had a very bright student named Martin who was very well liked by his peers and his professors. In jest, he was often called "Smarty Marty." Although he could have seen this as a put-down, Martin always took it in good spirit and never became angry. It isn't just what's said (for example, dopey, silly, baldy, geeky, or shorty) that creates anger but also how the recipient sees it. Anger emerges when such teasing statements are seen as demeaning and disrespectful. How you judge the intentions of others makes all the difference in whether or not you become angry.

As it turns out, there are some common thinking patterns that lead to anger. These patterns were first identified by psychologist Dr. Albert Ellis and psychiatrist Dr. Aaron Beck, who developed a successful treatment called "cognitive therapy." See if you recognize any of the following patterns in your own anger experiences.

Awfulizing. This type of thinking involves exaggeration. Daily hassles are described as *awful, horrible,* or *terrible* when, in fact, they're ordinary and manageable. Awfulizing leads to complaints about how incredibly bad the problem is, which wastes time and effort for productive problem solving. Putting your energy into creating solutions is better than exaggerating and whining about circumstances you don't like. Plus, nobody wants to hang around someone who endlessly exaggerates and gripes about their problems.

Low frustration tolerance. People who think this way underestimate their ability to deal with misfortunes. Adversities, instead of being viewed as a normal part of life or challenges to face, are seen as situations that you *can't stand, can't take,* or *can't tolerate.*

It's useful to note that there's a relationship between awfulizing and low frustration tolerance. When you think of a situation as awful or catastrophic, you're less likely to believe you can tolerate it. In spite of their own bluster, people who think this way typically *do* tolerate the situations they complain about.

Bettina used to say, "I just can't take it when my kids bicker with each other." Nevertheless, she took it for the next ten years until they went off to college. John used to say, "My boss treats me horribly. I can't take him anymore." Nevertheless, he stayed on the job for another twenty-one years. Finally, Seymour used to say, "I have so much trouble at home. My wife doesn't keep the house clean. The kids are out of control. My computer is always broken, and my car is about to go to the junkyard. I can't stand my life." Nevertheless, he remained with his family for the rest of his life.

Bettina, John, and Seymour talked as if they couldn't cope with the struggles in their lives. But the reality was that they did tolerate their lives and they did handle their problems for many years.

What about you? Do you awfulize, moan about misfortunes, and believe you aren't capable of handling life's problems? Or do you see your difficulties as interesting challenges to be met?

Demandingness. Believing that other people *must* act the way you want them to act is called "demandingness." Said another way, it's taking your own personal views and elevating them to rules you impose on other people and the world around you. Of course, we all sometimes wish that others would behave the way we'd like. We also might *want* the world to conform to our personal desires. However, there's a difference between wanting different behavior from others and demanding it. Demandingness shows up when you use terms like "should, must, ought to," and "have to." Are you a demander? Or do you accept the fact that a lot of things in your life won't go the way you'd like?

Negative, global ratings of others. In this type of thinking, you see the person who instigated your anger in extreme terms. This involves condemning that person's total existence based on a few actions. For example, if you have a disagreement with a friend or family member you might think to yourself, "Who the hell is she to tell me what to do? She's a total moron. I don't want anything to do with her." Most people you love or like will at some point disappoint you. Thinking about others in extreme terms will surely fuel your anger and make it difficult for you to resolve problems and maintain relationships.

Another example would be saying the following things to yourself in response to an inconsiderate driver, "He should get the hell out of the passing lane. Jerk! What an ass." In this type of situation, you have very little information about the other driver. If you're honest with yourself, you'd probably acknowledge you haven't always been a perfect driver; but you wouldn't describe yourself with such negative terms when you make mistakes. You find negative ratings of others in statements like "He's just a . . . ," "She's a total . . . ," or "What a jerk/fool/dope he or she is."

Does this sound like you? Do you totally condemn others even though you know they do both good and bad things? Or do you separate individual actions from total ratings of others?

Negative, global ratings of self. As noted in the section on triggers, you might blame or condemn yourself when things don't go well. In your mind, you harshly criticize yourself and put yourself down when things don't go your way. You might say to yourself, "I'm a loser. I can't do anything right" or "I'll never succeed." If this is one of your thought patterns, you probably experience guilt, shame, and sadness along with anger.

Misinterpretations and distortions. During times of anger, your evaluations of other people's motives and intentions are more likely to be distorted or exaggerated. For example, thirty-three-year-old Friedrich viewed his in-laws' frequent phone calls and visits as "totally intrusive." As a result, he often felt angry with them. He believed the calls and visits were motivated by a lack of trust in him and a desire to check up on their daughter. Upon closer examination, it became clear that his in-laws just enjoyed spending time with their children and grandchildren. The motivations Friedrich attributed to his in-laws were distortions of their intentions. The tendency to misunderstand the behavior of others or distort what is going on is especially common when situations are ambiguous.

How clearly do you assess situations when you're angry? Have there been times when your thoughts about an event were completely off the mark?

Now, return to the anger event you identified earlier. This time, we'd like you to think about the thoughts you had during or immediately after the anger episode. If you have trouble identifying thoughts, look at the Evaluations box and try to recognize the ideas you held when you were angry. Place a check mark next to all the thoughts you had. It's OK to check more than one thought.

Evaluations

Check each thought that you had about the trigger.

____ *Awfulizing* (I thought this was one of the worst things that could be happening.)

____ *Low frustration tolerance* (I thought I could not handle or deal with this situation.)

____ *Demandingness* (I thought the other person absolutely should have acted differently.)

____ *Other-rating* (I thought the other person was "bad . . . worthless . . . a real #@*%&.")

____ *Self-rating* (Deep down, I thought I was less important or worthwhile.)

____ *Distortion* (My thinking became distorted; I didn't see things clearly.)

Personal Experiences

As mentioned in chapter 1, anger is something you feel inside. The experiences part of the model refers to your awareness of how strong your anger is, how long it lasts, and how it feels physically. Think about the anger event you identified earlier. Using the Personal Experiences box, you'll now focus on several aspects of your anger experience. Use the following characteristics as a guide.

Anger intensity. This is your rating of the strength of your anger. We find it helpful to rate anger on a 0 to 100 scale, where 0 means no anger and 100 represents the most anger you've ever experienced. When making your rating, consider how upset you felt, how extreme your thoughts were, how out of control you felt at the time, and the actions you wanted to take. A lot of folks find it useful to use our Anger Thermometer, which appears on page 32. It contains a series of words that allows you to judge how intense your anger was. Also, as you familiarize yourself with these words, you'll develop an emotional vocabulary so you can describe the intensity of your anger to others.

Duration. As you remember the anger episode, make your best estimate of how long the anger lasted. If the situation is ongoing and you continue to feel angry about it, indicate how long you've been angry and check the box that says "still ongoing."

Sensations you feel in your body. People experience a wide variety of physical symptoms when angry. These include increased heart rate, sweating, muscle tension, headaches, upset stomach, and shaking. In fact, rapid heart rate, muscle tension, and trembling are among the most commonly reported physical symptoms of anger. Place a check next to each of the physical sensations that were present for the anger episode. It isn't unusual to experience multiple physical sensations; so it's OK to place a check next to more than one item.

Personal Experiences

Rate your anger intensity level and the duration of your anger, and check those physical sensations that you noticed.

How intense was your anger in this situation?

0 | | | | | | | | | 100
none   mild   moderate   strong   extreme

How long did your anger last?

___ minutes ___ hours ___ days ___ still ongoing

What physical sensations did you experience? (check as many as apply)

___ Muscle tension	___ Fluttering in stomach	___ Sweating
___ Rapid heart rate	___ Nausea	___ Indigestion
___ Headache	___ Rapid breathing	___ Diarrhea
___ Upset Stomach	___ Tingling sensations	___ Positive energy
___ Flushing	___ Feelings of unreality	___ Fatigue
___ Trembling	___ Dizziness	

One goal of anger management is to be able to express your feelings directly to another person, with a word that expresses the true intensity of your feeling. There is no point in exaggerating or minimizing what you feel. Our thermometer can help you develop an anger vocabulary so you can appropriately communicate feelings of annoyance, anger, and rage. It's important to know that proper expression of anger never includes threats of aggression. As a rule, appropriate anger is of mild to moderate intensity and can be expressed simply by saying, "I feel...."

Consider the problem you're dealing with, and examine the words listed below. Then complete the following sentence:

"When I consider this specific event, I feel/felt _____"

100° Rabid — Crazed — Maniacal — Wild — Violent — Demented

90° Frenzied — Vicious — Unhinged — Untuned — Up in arms

80° Incensed — Infuriated/Furious — Enraged — Hysterical

70° Irate — Inflamed — Exasperated — Fuming — Burned up

60° Fired up — Riled up — All worked up — Peeved — Indignant — Nuts

50° Mad — Angry — Agitated — Pissed off — Irked — Aggravated

40° Provoked — Impelled — Cranky — Crotchety — Distressed — Disturbed

30° Annoyed — Bothered — Irritated — Perturbed — Flustered — Uneasy

20° Jogged — Moved — Stirred — Ruffled — Challenged

10° Aroused — Actuated — Alert — Awakened — Kindled

0° Sleeping — Dead — Comatose

Kassinove and Tafrate's Anger Thermometer

Expressive Patterns

The next step is to see which expressive patterns or actions fit your personal experience of anger best. There are a lot of ways people express themselves when angry. The most common are listed below. Use the list to help you see which patterns are similar to yours, and then complete the Expressive Patterns box. If you did something that isn't mentioned, you can write it in the space labeled "other."

Holding anger in. Some people tend to keep their anger inside. For example, although you're aware of your anger, you might decide that it's too risky to show it. If you work hard to hide your anger, you might still have angry thoughts and you might brood about the problem. Holding your anger in can result from passivity and lack of assertiveness. In addition, you might hold long-term grudges that keep you from solving your problems.

Indirect anger expression. Some people — and maybe you're one of them — express their anger indirectly. This includes destroying property; ruining social or work relationships; gossiping or spreading misinformation to harm the targets of your anger; passively resisting demands to perform at expected levels in jobs and relationships; not following rules; not carrying your weight on team projects; and not responding to requests made by romantic partners or other important people in your life.

Outward expression — verbal. The most common way to express anger is verbally. This includes the following: yelling, accusing, threatening, cursing, arguing, demanding, making nasty remarks, and using sarcasm.

Outward expression — physical. Physical reactions are less common than verbal reactions; however, physical actions are likely to result in more serious consequences. These behaviors include hitting, kicking, shoving, throwing or breaking objects, slamming doors, and destroying property.

Outward expression — gestures. Another common way that anger is expressed is through some type of body movement. This includes rolling your eyes, crossing your arms, glaring, frowning, pouting, and "giving the finger" to others.

Avoidance. Some people work hard to not experience anger. When they do, they choose to avoid or withdraw from situations and people. Distracting activities such as watching TV, listening to music, reading books, and playing video games can be used to avoid the experience of anger.

Alcohol and drug use. Another behavior that appears in connection with angry feelings and thoughts is the use of alcohol or other drugs (prescription and nonprescription). As we noted in chapter 1, substance use is one of the most common problems that overlap with

---

Expressive Patterns

(Check each behavior that was connected with your anger.)

___ *Held anger in* (kept things in; boiled inside; harbored grudges)

___ *Indirectly expressed anger* (did something secretly harmful to the person, spread rumors or gossip, or deliberately did not follow rules.)

___ *Outward expression — Verbal* (yelled, screamed, argued, threatened, made sarcastic, nasty, or abusive remarks)

___ *Outward expression — Physical* (fought, hit, kicked, pushed, or shoved someone; broke, threw, slammed, or destroyed an object)

___ *Outward expression — Bodily gestures* (rolled eyes, crossed arms, glared, frowned, gave a stern look)

___ *Avoidance* (escaped or withdrew from the situation; distracted myself by reading, watching TV, or listening to music)

___ *Substance use* (drank beer/alcohol; took medications such as aspirin, valium, etc.; took other drugs such as marijuana, cocaine, etc.)

___ *Tried to resolve the situation* (compromised, discussed, or came to some agreement with the person)

___ *Other:* _____

---

anger. Using alcohol or drugs to cope with your anger helps you avoid your problems in the short term but is likely to create other difficulties in the long run.

Attempts to resolve the situation. Anger, as we noted earlier, isn't always bad and can sometimes lead to problem resolution. When angry, people sometimes want to compromise, cool down, and try to come up with solutions to problems. Indeed, there have probably been times when anger has energized you to face a problem or deal with a difficult situation.

Outcomes

Every anger episode results in some type of "outcome." Outcomes are a critical part of the anger episode model. Angry behavior that has typically been followed by something good — such as attention, compliance, and admiration — is likely to reappear in the future. Angry behavior that hasn't typically been followed by anything good — as when it's ignored — is unlikely to reappear. Angry behavior that has been punished — such as being fired or arrested — might be suppressed. So the outcomes that follow your angry behavior influence whether the angry behavior will be repeated in the future.

You can think of your anger episodes as leading to both short-term and long-term outcomes. Short-term outcomes appear either during the anger episode or shortly afterward and have the greatest likelihood of affecting your angry behavior, because consequences close in time have the most powerful effects.

One possible short-term outcome involves the behavior of other people, as when your wife or husband, child, or employee immediately complies with your angry demands. Another outcome is the release of two chemicals — epinephrine and cortisol — which produce a surge of energy. Your heart rate, blood pressure, and breathing increase, your body temperature rises, and your skin perspires. Your mind is sharpened and focused. In a situation where you might have first felt demeaned and powerless, there's now a feeling of power from the chemical rush. Feeling strong anger provides the illusion of being capable and in control of situations you used to think caused you problems. So your anger is rewarded, in the short term, by chemical reactions that take place in your body as well as by the behaviors of others.

The long-term outcomes connected to your anger appear after the anger episode has ended. Although these long-term outcomes are generally undesirable, some are good. Some people tell us that anger has made them successful on the job and that others always know where they stand on difficult issues. A lifetime of being angry does have occasional benefits.

However, people who have reacted with anger for a long time tend to experience a lot of bad long-term outcomes. For some people, and you might fit into this category, anger doesn't just energize behavior — it disrupts behavior. Anger doesn't improve communication — it threatens others. Anger doesn't just result in feeling more powerful in difficult situations — it instigates aggressive behavior. Some of the negative outcomes, however, might not appear for many years. Like the long-term effects of cigarette smoking, exposure to asbestos, or exposure to water pollution, these anger outcomes come only after years of agitation, argument, and discord. It might be difficult for you to see that these outcomes are linked to your anger, since they take so long to emerge. But rest assured, anger is a very real problem over the course of a lifetime.

Here is a short list of long-term outcomes that go along with anger:

- relationship and family conflict
- a poor reputation
- workplace problems, leading to lack of job advancement and being excluded from meetings
- bad decision making and increased risk taking, leading to business and personal failures
- physical injuries that require emergency room visits
- alcohol and drug abuse
- arrest and imprisonment
- poor concentration and lessened productivity, causing educational and work problems
- erratic driving habits
- a habit of aggression in reaction to normal difficulties
- high blood pressure, heart disease, and stroke

Outcomes

List the positive and negative outcomes of this anger episode.

Positive short-term outcomes:

_____

_____

_____

Positive long-term outcomes:

_____

_____

_____

Negative short-term outcomes:

_____

_____

_____

Negative long-term outcomes:

_____

_____

_____

Please return to the anger event you identified earlier. We'd like you to consider the outcomes that are connected with this anger episode. First, consider the immediate or short-term effects. Try to think of both good and bad outcomes. Next, think about the long-term outcomes. To do this, you'll have to imagine how this anger event will likely affect your relationship with the person(s) involved and what the long-term results might be. Again, try to identify both good and bad potential outcomes. Use the Outcomes box for this part of the exercise.

CONCLUSION AND A SMALL HOMEWORK ASSIGNMENT

Congratulations! By analyzing one of your anger episodes, you've taken the first step toward gaining better control over your reactions. To make this really useful, however, it's important that you examine three or four additional anger events. You need to analyze several anger episodes to identify which patterns are most common and important for you.

On pages 40 and 41, we've provided an Anger Episode Record Self-Report Form. It combines all the sections you just completed. Make a few copies of the form and use them to examine additional anger episodes. This task will increase your awareness of your anger patterns and will give you insight into some important questions, such as:

- Do my anger episodes usually start with the same type of trigger?
- When angry, what am I usually thinking?
- When angry, what do I usually do?
- How does my anger get rewarded?
- What effect does my anger have on my relationships over the long run?

Answers to these questions will be useful as you move forward with this program and learn how to use our seven proven techniques to reduce your anger. Once you've completed two or three of these records, proceed to the next chapter.

We think it's great that you've begun to read this book. We also recognize that you might not yet be fully committed to dealing with your anger. In the next chapter, therefore, we help you look at the pros and cons of improving the way you act when you're angry. Skip that chapter if you're already strongly motivated and are ready to work toward change. If you're hesitant, we hope to help you clarify your own reasons for working to improve this part of your life.

KEY POINTS TO REMEMBER

- Anger episodes follow a predictable pattern: triggers, evaluations, personal experiences, patterns of expression, and outcomes.

- The most common trigger for anger is the undesirable behavior of people you know well and like.

- Anger typically emerges when you distort the trigger or exaggerate its meaning.

- Demandingness is the belief that other people must act the way you want them to. This is a common belief that's held when anger emerges. Be alert for it.

- Personal anger experiences vary in frequency, intensity, and duration. Ask yourself how often you become angry, how strong your feeling is, and how long it lasts?

- Anger can be expressed in many ways. The most frequent are verbal behaviors such as yelling, arguing, cursing, and making nasty remarks.

- The long-term outcomes of anger seem to be the most serious. Consider the long-term damage that anger might lead to in your relationships, health, and happiness.

- Increasing your awareness and understanding of anger episodes is an important first step toward anger control.

- Analyze a few of your anger events using the Anger Episode Record Self-Report Form.

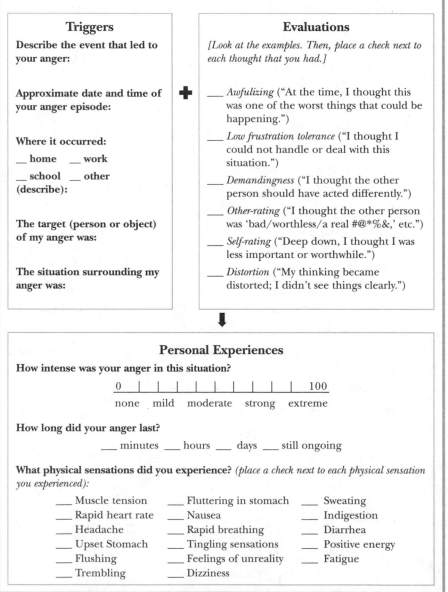

Anger Episode Record Self-Report Form

Triggers + Evaluations → **Personal Experiences** → **Expressive Patterns** → **Outcomes**

Directions: Fill out one record for each episode of anger you experience. Provide information in each box.

Triggers

Describe the event that led to your anger:

Approximate date and time of your anger episode:

Where it occurred:
__ home __ work
__ school __ other
(describe):

The target (person or object) of my anger was:

The situation surrounding my anger was:

Evaluations

[Look at the examples. Then, place a check next to each thought that you had.]

___ *Awfulizing* ("At the time, I thought this was one of the worst things that could be happening.")

___ *Low frustration tolerance* ("I thought I could not handle or deal with this situation.")

___ *Demandingness* ("I thought the other person should have acted differently.")

___ *Other-rating* ("I thought the other person was 'bad/worthless/a real #@*%&,' etc.")

___ *Self-rating* ("Deep down, I thought I was less important or worthwhile.")

___ *Distortion* ("My thinking became distorted; I didn't see things clearly.")

Personal Experiences

How intense was your anger in this situation?

0 | | | | | | | | | | 100
none mild moderate strong extreme

How long did your anger last?

___ minutes ___ hours ___ days ___ still ongoing

What physical sensations did you experience? *(place a check next to each physical sensation you experienced):*

___ Muscle tension	___ Fluttering in stomach	___ Sweating
___ Rapid heart rate	___ Nausea	___ Indigestion
___ Headache	___ Rapid breathing	___ Diarrhea
___ Upset Stomach	___ Tingling sensations	___ Positive energy
___ Flushing	___ Feelings of unreality	___ Fatigue
___ Trembling	___ Dizziness	

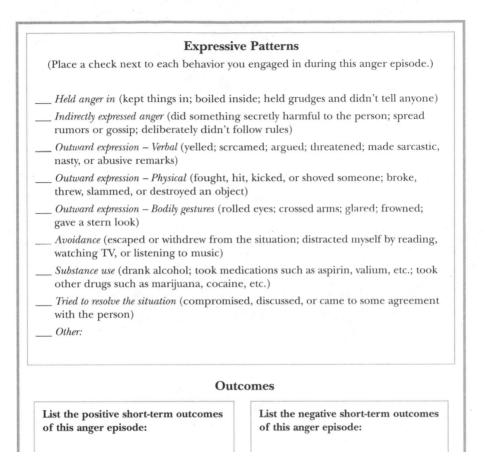

Expressive Patterns

(Place a check next to each behavior you engaged in during this anger episode.)

___ *Held anger in* (kept things in; boiled inside; held grudges and didn't tell anyone)

___ *Indirectly expressed anger* (did something secretly harmful to the person; spread rumors or gossip; deliberately didn't follow rules)

___ *Outward expression – Verbal* (yelled; screamed; argued; threatened; made sarcastic, nasty, or abusive remarks)

___ *Outward expression – Physical* (fought, hit, kicked, or shoved someone; broke, threw, slammed, or destroyed an object)

___ *Outward expression – Bodily gestures* (rolled eyes; crossed arms; glared; frowned; gave a stern look)

___ *Avoidance* (escaped or withdrew from the situation; distracted myself by reading, watching TV, or listening to music)

___ *Substance use* (drank alcohol; took medications such as aspirin, valium, etc.; took other drugs such as marijuana, cocaine, etc.)

___ *Tried to resolve the situation* (compromised, discussed, or came to some agreement with the person)

___ *Other:*

Outcomes

List the positive short-term outcomes of this anger episode:	**List the negative short-term outcomes of this anger episode:**

List the positive long-term outcomes of this anger episode:	**List the negative long-term outcomes of this anger episode:**

CHAPTER 3

ARE YOU READY TO CHANGE?

There's only one corner of the universe you can be certain of improving, and that's your own self.

— ALDOUS HUXLEY, writer

Changing how you react to the unwanted events of life requires more than hope and thought. It requires energy and effort. Just reading this book without practicing the new skills isn't enough. A lot of folks say, "I want to stop yelling and screaming. I know it's bad for me and my family" or "I always feel so tense and frustrated. I'd like to let things go more easily." We've learned that even when people are thinking about changing the way they act when they're angry, it doesn't mean that they're ready to do the work that leads to better anger control.

By the end of this chapter, you'll be able to clearly state your reasons for either wanting to reduce your anger or for staying as you are. You'll understand your level of readiness and motivation to work on your anger. We invite you to think about your life, to answer some personal questions, and to write down your answers. If you don't want to write the information in the boxes, that's OK. Just think about how you'd answer each question. As we said in chapter 2, if you're already sure that your anger is a problem and you're ready to work on anger reduction, you can skip to the next chapter. However, you'll likely find it useful to consider the ideas we present here.

First, please look at the stories of Alan and Sarah. Anger caused both of them problems in their lives. Alan's story shows someone who ignored his problems and held onto his anger for his entire life.

Sarah's story shows a person who experienced anger-related problems but eventually developed self-awareness and a commitment to change.

It's Your Choice

Obviously, everybody's life is different. Your own experiences are unique, and since we're not seeing you in person, we can't fully understand your

Alan: The Exploder

Alan was a married man with two grown children. In his younger years, he was known to have an explosive temper. His outbursts, which included yelling and breaking furniture, scared his family. For years, his wife and children tiptoed around the house in order not to upset him. Alan's anger wasn't confined to his family. He had frequent conflicts at work, ended several friendships over minor disagreements, and harbored grudges against those he thought had treated him badly. This pattern continued for many years. Then, as he got older, he developed a number of serious health problems, including high blood pressure and irritable bowel syndrome. His wife and friends urged Alan to get help for his anger, but he refused. Although he admitted to "feeling stressed out" a lot of the time, Alan insisted that it was "other people" who caused him to react with anger.

He refused to look inside himself and examine the role he played in shaping his emotional responses. Eventually, Alan's children grew up and moved out of the house. Predictably, they remained distant and wary of dealing with him. Alan complained about their lack of attention. Although his wife stayed in the marriage, she grew more independent and spent increasingly more time with friends, who she considered more positive and supportive. As time went along, his friends and co-workers simply ignored him. After years of angry outbursts and bitterness, Alan finally came in for anger management counseling. Even then, he wasn't open-minded about changing the ways he reacted. Rather, he wanted to spend the session time complaining about how others were unfair to him and how *they* should change. Alan never developed a true appreciation of the damage that his anger caused to his relationships with family, friends, and co-workers. He died of a high blood pressure related stroke at age sixty-three.

Sarah: The Bickerer

Sarah was thirty-eight, divorced, and shared custody of her eight-year-old son with her ex-husband. Constant quarrelling marked her first marriage. Sarah believed that her ex-husband was almost always responsible for their arguments. She  later married a man who had a seven-year-old daughter, and her second marriage went well for the first few months. However, over time she found that she was frequently arguing with her new husband. The conflicts became more heated, and Sarah began to doubt whether this new marriage would last. As the fighting increased, her son became depressed and withdrawn, and her stepdaughter had tantrums at home and in school.

After talking with a friend, Sarah came to the painful realization that she herself bore some of the responsibility for the yelling and arguing in both marriages. She also recognized that she didn't want to go through another divorce and didn't want her young son to experience any more loss. She was determined to learn how to create a calm and stable home life for herself and her family. Sarah sought counseling, was motivated throughout the course of her anger management sessions, and was successful in changing the way she behaved when she was angry. Although there were still occasional arguments, they weren't as destructive as past arguments. Sarah learned to not react so quickly when things went wrong and to adapt to difficult and challenging situations more easily. This led to greater peace in the household, and the behavior of both children improved.

anger. But *you* can! We ask you to look at yourself honestly and decide whether it's time to live your life with less anger.

The reality is that we *all* experience unfairness and bad treatment from others. How you choose to react to mistreatment will determine how angry you get, which, in turn, influences the quality of your life. When things go badly, you can certainly get angry. It's your choice. But as we discuss later, anger isn't the only option for dealing with the difficulties of life. You can decide if your anger is too strong and if it's helpful to you. Although other people might be pressuring you to reduce your anger, no one can really force you to make a change.

You have the capacity to examine your circumstances and decide what to do.

REASONS TO CHANGE AND REASONS TO STAY THE SAME

What's happening in your life right now that's leading you to think about a change? Perhaps you're motivated to reduce your angry reactions because you know that others suffer when you yell, scream, withdraw, or pout. Maybe your reactions have led to work, family, friendship, or health problems or even problems with the law. These problems might be serving as a wake-up call to tell you change is necessary. Maybe a counselor has asked you to read this book as part of an educational or intervention program. All of these are external reasons.

In contrast, wanting to change can come simply from wanting a more comfortable life and knowing that you can achieve it. You might want to reduce your anger to create a calmer and more peaceful home life, like Sarah, make your relationships with friends and family more fulfilling, or improve your chances for career advancement. There are really two parts to the motivation equation:

1. recognition that your current anger reactions aren't working
2. the ability to see a better way of reacting to life's difficulties

Of course, some people (like Alan) choose not to change. Such people don't see the downside to their anger. They think of their anger as perfectly appropriate. After all, they say, "Wouldn't you be very angry if your child didn't listen to you/your husband kept looking at other women/your wife kept wasting money/your friend didn't keep his promises/your good advice was ignored," and so on. It's so important to them to see their anger as appropriate that they fail to ask themselves if it helps to solve their problems. Creating excuses to keep being angry is easy.

As it turns out, most people think along the same lines when they experience anger. We've already noted that when people are angry they typically believe that they've been neglected, ignored, or treated unfairly, that someone else has acted wrongly, that the other person could have acted better if he or she really wanted to, that the unfair treatment was awful or terrible, or that they can't tolerate or deal with the misfortunes. These thoughts keep anger going. They focus on the other person as the wrongdoer and you as the righteous one. These thoughts, however, don't help you examine the consequences of your anger.

Some people are concerned about their anger but don't think they can change. They use stubborn acceptance of their current state and denial of their ability to change as a way to avoid making the effort. They say, "Yeah, my anger sometimes gets me in trouble, but it's no big deal. My wife/son/friends/co-workers know that's the kind of person I am. I can't help being angry. It's who I am."

The Big Mistake

Angry people who have the kinds of thoughts listed above, which focus on others' bad behavior, aren't very concerned about their own actions. They spend lifetimes playing the "blame game." After all, if the other person is at fault and is the cause of your anger, why should you have to change anything? Focusing on the misdeeds of others (no matter how awful they might be) allows you to think holding on to anger is just fine. Regrettably, no matter how moral, proper, warranted, excusable, or justified your anger might seem, it rarely leads to beneficial changes in others. This big mistake — focusing exclusively on the bad behavior of others — will do away with any desire in you to learn to react differently. Blaming others simply doesn't help!

Ambivalence

You might be ambivalent about fully committing to changing your anger. On the one hand, you might recognize the personal pain and costs that accompany it (for example, crummy relations with your husband or wife or children). On the other hand, you might have seemingly good reasons and excuses to remain angry ("If he really cared for me, he wouldn't treat me this way"). It's completely normal to feel both ways about your angry reactions.

Ambivalence actually means feeling two ways about something. A lot of people, for example, have both wanted and not wanted to stop smoking at the very same time. Others have both wanted and not wanted to go on a diet, to reduce their drinking, to change jobs, to move, to end their marriage, and so on. They go back and forth, trying to decide what to do — *being ambivalent.* This type of wavering is normal and is to be expected when you first consider changing long-standing behaviors, emotions, or situations.

As psychologists, we've seen ambivalence and indecisiveness in people who are struggling with all sorts of difficulties. Few people with anger problems arrive in our office totally committed to change. Rather, they're ambivalent. They usually have good reasons to keep being angry. At the same time, they have compelling reasons to reduce their angry reactions. The trick is to understand your own reasons on both sides of the "Should I deal with my anger?" issue and to make a decision about what's in your best interests over the long run.

Now, let's take a closer look at this issue. By understanding your ambivalence about anger reduction, you'll get a better picture of where you stand. We certainly recognize that anger has some benefits and that there are reasons *not* to change and to continue being angry. These are example responses from people we've worked with:

- It feels good to vent my angry feelings. I feel better when I let it out!
- If I don't get angry, others will walk all over me.
- Anger helps me get what I want.
- When they treat me badly, my anger helps me express myself.
- Anger is one way to send a message that you shouldn't mess with me.
- What else are you supposed to feel when they disrespect you? My anger is appropriate!
- Anger gives me a feeling of power, and I like that.
- When I get angry, I give people just what they deserve!

First, we would like you to consider the positive side of the way you act when you're angry. Write your ideas in the box, "Reasons to *Keep* My

Angry Feelings and Reactions." Don't worry about how many ideas you come up with. Just identify the major reasons for keeping your anger as it is now.

Reasons to *Keep* My Angry Feelings and Reactions

_____

_____

_____

_____

OK, now let's look at the other side — the reasons to make a change in your reactions and to reduce your anger. As we've noted in the previous chapters, there are quite a few reasons to change. For you, these might include

- improving relationships with your wife or husband, children, and friends
- increasing your effectiveness at work
- having closer family ties
- wanting less chaos in your life
- saving your marriage
- reducing the chances of problems with the law
- lessening the effects of physical health problems

Think about what your anger costs you. Don't consider only the most recent or most dramatic anger episodes and problems; also consider the more subtle and long-term consequences you've experienced. Obviously, these results represent the negative side of the way you act when you're angry and are potential reasons for making a change. Write these items in the box, "Reasons to Bring My Angry Feelings and Reactions under Control." As before, focus on the most important reasons for making a change in your life.

Reasons to Bring My Angry Feelings and Reactions under Control

_____

_____

_____

_____

By this point, you'll have reasons in both boxes. Keep in mind that this isn't about the number of items you've listed in each box. Rather, it's simply a way of clearly seeing your own reasons for and against managing your anger. As you look at your reasons, take into account that it's common for one or two items on either side of the equation to be more important or to carry more weight than all of the others. We've met people for whom just one reason was sufficient to set change in motion.

Examining the reasons to bring your angry feelings and reactions under control is the first step in resolving your ambivalence. Now that you've identified your thoughts on both sides of the issue, it's time to consider how important change is for you.

IMPORTANCE

How important is it for you to reduce your anger? Be thoughtful as you consider this question. Other people might have already complained that your anger drives them away, makes them feel uncomfortable, or causes disruptions in work and social relationships. Although it's valuable to consider what others say, your view is what matters the most. When answering the next set of questions, consider how *often* you become angry, how *intense* your reactions are, and how *long* your anger experiences last.

OK, considering your personal situation, rate how important you think it is to change the way you act when you're angry. In the box, circle a number on the 1 to 7 scale that best describes how important anger control is for you.

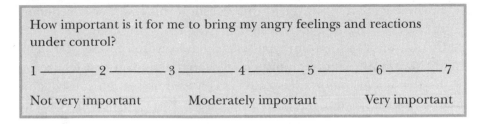

How important is it for me to bring my angry feelings and reactions under control?

1 ———— 2 ———— 3 ———— 4 ———— 5 ———— 6 ———— 7

Not very important   Moderately important   Very important

If your importance rating is a 2 or less, reducing your anger isn't a high priority for you. It's unlikely that at this time you'll have enough motivation to learn the materials and do the work we suggest. It might be better if you put this book away for a while and spend some time observing your reactions to the minor annoyances, rejections, disappointments, unfair treatment, and general hassles that are part of life. Also, examine your reactions to any major problems you experience. Pay attention to whether your anger is satisfying and whether it brings about the results you want. Examine the short-term outcomes of your anger as well as the likely long-term effects on you and others. Does anger work for you? If you're not sure, keep in mind that motivation isn't constant. Rather, it ebbs and flows. Therefore, even if you aren't motivated to work on your anger now, you might well feel different down the road.

If your importance rating is a 3, 4, or 5, you're moderately committed to reducing your anger. It's likely that there will be periods when you'll focus on the tasks in this program. At other times, you might put the required work on the back burner. Most people who struggle with anger rate themselves in this range. If this is you, we suggest you continue to read further. It's likely you can use this program effectively.

Now, think about a tricky question. Using the next box, ask yourself why your importance rating wasn't lower.

Why is my *importance* rating not lower (like a 1)?

_____

_____

_____

Surprisingly, your answer to this question will reveal why reducing your anger is important. After all, if you really thought that anger reduction wasn't important, you would have given a rating of 1. This might show you're more motivated to change than you first realized.

If your initial importance rating was a 6 or 7, you obviously think that a change in your behavior is essential. You're probably ready to commit yourself to learning and completing this program. Keep in mind that even though your commitment to change is high, your motivation can still fluctuate. Now answer the question in the next box.

Why is my importance rating at the high end of the scale?

_____

_____

_____

Again, your answer is likely to provide a clear reason why making a reduction in your angry feelings and reactions is important. As you read through (or reread) each chapter, remind yourself of why completing this program is in line with what you think is important in life and with your goals for improving your life.

READINESS

Why now? Although you might now recognize that it's important to reduce your anger, you might or might not think that this is the time to

do it. Some people have told us that they're not ready to work on their anger because they don't believe they have the time or the energy to give it their best effort. We agree that timing is important. Certainly, it might be unwise to consider using this guidebook if you have too many pressing commitments and obligations. On the other hand, conditions are rarely perfect.

You might be telling yourself you can work on anger reduction at a later time. On the surface, it often appears easier to not face problems and to put things off. In actuality, not facing problems is much more difficult in the long run. The energy and effort required to manage your life with the problem-causing ways you behave when you're angry and the resulting chaos are usually far greater than the energy and effort required to reduce your anger.

We recognize that wanting to put things off is normal. Take smoking for example. It's common for smokers to tell themselves that they'll quit at some point in the future. We've worked with adults who say, "I plan to quit smoking as soon as I get a job/complete my college degree/get married/become pregnant," etc. Excessive drinkers, drug users, and overweight adults say the same things. Procrastinators of all sorts acknowledge the importance of change, but their commitment in the present moment just isn't there. The good news is that, over time, the arguments for dealing with problems often become stronger and people eventually take the necessary steps to make their lives better. The key is to change *before* the difficulties your behavior has caused create severe problems in your life.

So how ready are you to work on your anger? Consider the question in the box, "How *ready* am I to change my angry feelings and reactions" and circle the number on the 1 to 7 scale that best describes where you are right now.

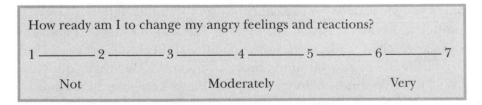

If your readiness rating was in the area of 1 or 2, you don't have a strong desire to bring your anger under control at the present time. Try to figure out if it's just having too many current commitments or if you're avoiding facing your anger problems. If you believe that you're truly too busy, find a time in the future when you can give our program a reasonable effort. But if you think your lack of readiness has more to do with avoidance, ask yourself the following question: "What would

have to happen to make me more ready to change my anger reactions?"
Write your answer in the next box.

> What would have to happen to make me more ready to change my anger
> reactions?
>
> _____
>
> _____
>
> _____

Discomfort and recognition that there's a problem often instigates
change. It's possible that your anger hasn't led to much loss or pain.
Thus, your anger might not seem to be much of a problem. Perhaps
your marriage still seems intact and, although you haven't progressed at
work, at least you haven't been fired. Perhaps your friends are still with
you, although they might have become more like distant acquaintances.
And perhaps you're blaming the problems with your children on the
school or their friends, rather than recognizing your part in them.
Your answer to the above question reveals the types of losses or costs
that are meaningful to you and that could influence your decision to
work on anger control. Only you can decide if the right time is now.

A readiness rating of 3, 4, or 5 indicates that there are clear times
when you see your anger as a concern. At other times, it doesn't seem to
bother you as much. Again, most people fall into this middle range and
can expect their readiness to work on anger control to waver somewhat.
To clarify the issue a bit more, again ask yourself our tricky question,
"Why is my readiness rating not lower?" Put your answer in the box.

> Why is my readiness rating not lower (like a 1)?
>
> _____
>
> _____
>
> _____

Your answer will highlight why change *is* important now. After all, if you didn't think that working on your anger was somewhat pressing, you would have given a lower rating. As you examine your life and look ahead, it's worthwhile to be aware of why reducing anger might be urgent. Recognition of the costs of your anger will increase your readiness to work on it.

If your readiness rating is a 6 or 7, now is clearly the time to commit to this program. This is a case where it's important to "strike while the iron is hot." Again, let's make sure your reasoning is crystal clear by looking at the box that asks, "Why is my readiness rating at the high end of the scale?" Your answer will clarify the concerns that have brought you to the point of being ready to pursue change.

Why is my readiness rating at the high end of the scale?

_____

_____

_____

CONCLUSION

There are a lot of good reasons to reduce frequent, intense, and long-term anger reactions and a few to stay as you are. We ask you to examine your life to see if anger works for you. You don't have to be at a 6 or 7 on both the importance and readiness ratings for our program to be useful. Most people find themselves somewhere in the middle, and most will profit from learning our seven proven ways to manage anger and live a happier life. We simply think that it's helpful if you state your reasons for working toward anger control, and we hope that thinking about the questions we posed has given you clearer insight into your own arguments for change.

However, as we said, motivation levels fluctuate. Depending on the experiences you have during the next few weeks, your ratings could be different. Adults and teenagers with anger difficulties are often less motivated during periods of relative calm. Motivation quickly increases after experiencing a "blowup" that results in negative consequences, such as family disruption, the loss of a friendship or a job, or a run-in with the law. The best way to deal with these variations in motivation is to consider the *long-term* benefits of changing versus staying as you are.

In chapters 1 and 2, we provided you with basic information about anger and helped you to understand your own anger patterns more clearly. In this chapter, we helped you consider your own reasons to reduce your anger reactions. We hope that you are now ready to proceed to chapter 4, where you will be introduced to the first of the seven skills to better manage your anger.

KEY POINTS TO REMEMBER

- Even if others are pressuring you to be less angry, deciding to change is your choice.

- The "big mistake" is focusing exclusively on the bad behavior of others while ignoring the more important issue of whether your anger is working to make your life better.

- Ambivalence means feeling two ways about something. It's normal to be ambivalent about changing your anger.

- The energy required to manage your life with excessive and disruptive anger is far greater than the energy required to make a change.

- Consider what is at stake if you don't reduce your anger.

- Consider the three best reasons to reduce your angry feelings and reactions.

PART II

SEVEN PROVEN WAYS TO CONTROL ANGER

CHAPTER 4

AVOID AND ESCAPE

Every time you get angry, you poison your own system.
— ALFRED A. MONTAPERT, American author

Sometimes, there's little benefit to immediately facing the people or events that trigger your anger. In the short run, it might be better to avoid some people or situations until you develop additional skills to deal with them. This might seem like the easy way out. However, if you want to live a happy life, immediately confronting problems without forethought and planning is unwise. We suggest the use of "avoidance" and "escape" as a simple and concrete first step to help you break up angry patterns of behavior that have become automatic over time.

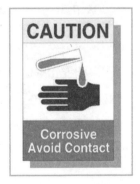

Avoidance and escape are different techniques. Avoidance refers to anticipating problems and intentionally not joining in with people or situations where you're likely to become angry. Escape refers to removing yourself from situations after problems have started and you notice that your anger is building.

Avoiding problems might initially seem weak or cowardly! Indeed, facing problems head-on and not hiding from life's difficulties is a desirable goal. We all know that it's important to talk to our children about bad grades, inappropriate friends, sex, drugs, and the like. We all know that eventually we'll have to talk to a husband or wife we suspect of having an affair, to a business partner who isn't carrying her or his load, to a friend who gossips, or to a neighbor who has loud parties late into the night. Here, our relationships with the other people are likely to continue for a long time, and an eventual resolution is important.

WHICH, WHEN, AND HOW

The questions in this chapter revolve around the key words "which," "when," and "how." With regard to "which," we ask you to consider whether *all* problems have to be addressed. Do you *have to* tell off a rude taxi driver you'll never see again? Do you *have to* confront a slow and unhelpful salesperson? *Must* you give a piece of your mind to a person who jumps in front of you in line? Is it *your job* to make drivers who cut you off on the road see the error of their ways? Although you might experience some annoyance in these situations, you'd be wise to decide if taking an angry action will accomplish anything. Issues that can be resolved and that might lead to better behavior in the future might certainly warrant your energy and time. However, if you'll never see the person again, you might be better off just walking away.

With regard to "when," the time to address a particular problem might not be at the moment when you feel the angriest. Too many people act

impulsively. When dealing with difficult people and situations, timing is important. Take Matt, a high school science teacher who struggled with the disruptive behavior of one of his students. One afternoon, after a disrespectful comment by the student, Matt finally decided that he'd had enough. In front of the entire class, he impulsively launched into a loud and bitter denunciation laced with profanity. This resulted in a formal reprimand, and a lot of parents and students lost confidence in his ability to manage the classroom. It would have been better if Matt had chosen to not react in the moment but to confront the problem at a later time, after he had time to cool off and consult with co-workers about how to deal with the student. When bad and potentially angering events happen, you have the ability to decide when it will be best to address them.

The "how" is related to the "when." We believe that it's best to delay reacting to unpleasant people and situations until you've mastered the techniques in the upcoming chapters. The "how" requires knowing specific social problem solving techniques. It consists of knowing "how" to think about unpleasant people and situations in ways that improve the way you act when you're angry. If it seems unlikely that the problems can be resolved, the best solution might be to know "how" to let it go. We also want you to know "how" to relax. We want you to use relaxation methods if you have to continue to experience annoying people (like Aunt Mabel, who continues to ignore you during the holidays) or situations (like long checkout lines in the supermarket). Finally, we want you to know "how" to assertively let others know you're angry in ways that will improve communication, rather than increase arguments.

Knowing "which" situations are worth dealing with, "when" to approach them, and "how" to deal with them is your best bet for moving toward a calmer and happier life. Since you might not yet have mastered our skills to reduce anger, avoidance and removal from problems — that "cowardly" solution — will provide temporary relief from anger.

THE PRACTICE OF AVOIDANCE

Some of the anger you experience is likely to occur in response to predictable triggers. For example, you might become angry when your children repeatedly resist doing their homework or their room is messy, when your husband or wife repeatedly asks the same accusatory questions, or when a co-worker calls again and again to ask for favors. If you can arrange to be absent from those situations, you decrease your chance of becoming angry. The anger cycle is delayed, and the  problem can be dealt with at a later time. Sometimes, of course, the avoidance will produce a degree of worry or guilt, as it did for Steven. His story is presented in the accompanying box. The anger is, nevertheless, temporarily avoided, and that's the tradeoff.

Avoidance strategies don't produce long-lasting results. And, they might even make problems worse if your thoughtful avoidance isn't explained. For example, if you decide not to attend a Labor Day barbeque at your friend Mitchell's house because you know that Gary will be there and you always argue with him, it would be best if you tell Mitchell why you aren't coming. The larger point is that temporary avoidance reduces anger that develops in response to known and predictable anger triggers. Avoidance will also give you more time to develop better responses and coping strategies.

This approach is similar to what a doctor often recommends for a patient with an allergy. If the patient is allergic to cat dander — but loves cats — the doctors says to avoid the allergen as much as possible — no cats in the house. During the period of avoidance, other medical techniques, such as desensitization injections and medications that provide long-term allergy relief, can be started. Similarly, anger avoidance is useful before other, long-term anger management strategies have been learned.

Steven: "My Mother Is Such a Pain!"

Steven was a married fifty-two-year-old elementary school teacher. He had two children and often coached their sports teams. An only child, his father had died ten years earlier and his eighty-two-year-old mother lived nearby in a small apartment. The process of aging had taken its toll on his mother. She was hard of hearing, making telephone conversations difficult, and her declining vision made it impossible for her to drive. Her ability to think clearly also declined. In conversations, she would often forget what Steven had said.

All of this led his mother to become highly dependent on Steven. She called him at least twice a day. He had to drive her to the supermarket, pay her bills, repair small items in her apartment or hire contractors to fix larger problems, remind her of the children's birthdays, and take her to the doctor and dentist. Her bad memory caused a lot of difficulties. On days that he had to work, she would call saying, "I forgot to tell you that I have to see the dentist this morning. Will you drive me?" or "I know we just went to the supermarket, but I forgot to buy ketchup.

(Cont'd.)

Steven: "My Mother Is Such a Pain!" *(Continued)*

Will you please go and get it for me?" She would send out checks for bills that he had already paid and would regularly call him at work, insisting that he come out of his classroom to talk to her. The school principal tolerated the disruption for a while, but eventually told Steven to fix the problem. Friction was also developing between him and his wife, who felt neglected and complained that he wasn't spending enough time with their children.

Steven had frequent, but unproductive arguments with his mother. He told her not to call him at work, insisted that she get a hearing aid, and required her to make a shopping list before he took her out. Unfortunately, she would forget a lot of what he said and the anger continued. He knew that he had to develop a long-term plan for her care. In the interim, he decided to use avoidance and escape strategies to relieve some of the pressure.

He posted a calendar on her refrigerator door with a sign indicating that he was unavailable on Monday to Friday from 8:00 AM until 4:00 PM. He also listed the days and times when he was unavailable because of coaching. He told her that they could talk to each other only once a day, at about 8:00 PM, and he no longer took her calls at work. To avoid the unproductive arguments, he also made it clear that when he visited her he would stay for only forty-five minutes. He also bought her an alarm to be worn around her neck to assure that she could alert emergency services in case of a problem. Although he initially felt some guilt because he was avoiding her calls, he knew that she was safe from harm until he could find a better situation. Once the plan was put in place, he noticed improvement in his relationships with his wife and kids and that he was more focused and productive at work. Eventually, he moved his mother into a nearby assisted living facility where she could be looked after full time.

You might be saying to yourself that sometimes avoidance is impossible. We agree! Nevertheless, some thoughtful avoidance on your part can often go a long way in preventing anger outbursts. Consider some of the following possibilities for putting avoidance into action.

Planned Avoidance

Identify a situation that has previously led you to become angry, and decide to avoid it. For example, do you become angry in crowded stores, when you have to wait for a long time in your doctor's office, when your young child spills food or leaves toys strewn around the house, or when you have to travel on crowded parkways or freeways?

Sometimes you can arrange your life to avoid these hassles. For example, to make it less likely that you'll have to wait too long, you

can see your doctor at her first appointment of the day. If you become angry upon seeing your children's toys scattered around the house, you could agree with your husband or wife that you will call when you're about to leave work so there will be time to clean up. Finally, to avoid the potential anger trigger of rush hour traffic, some employers will allow you to adjust your working hours or will allow you to work at home. Alternatively, you might be able to ask for a transfer to a location in a less congested area.

These examples might not apply to you, but almost everyone can occasionally avoid dinner engagements where there's likely to be an angry blowup. And sometimes arguments can be avoided by simply avoiding such questions as, "Who did you go out with last night?" "Do you plan to have your child Bar Mitzvahed?" "Which is the best church in town?" or "Don't you think the Democrats (or Republicans) are complete morons?"

Allison, for example, used planned avoidance to better manage family holidays. She and her husband lived across the country from her in-laws. For the first few years of their marriage, they would go for visits and would plan to stay for five or six days. A predictable pattern emerged. The first two days were usually enjoyable. However, by day three or four, tension between Allison and her mother-in-law would start to build. The visits always ended with something uncomfortable happening. After considering the pattern, Allison decided that it was best if the visits were kept to three days. That way, the time spent with her in-laws would be enjoyable, and angry blowups would be less likely to occur.

Avoidance by Time Delays

As noted earlier, impulsive reactions can make difficult situations and problems worse. It's often valuable to put in a time delay before responding to annoying people or situations. For example, you might be asked to do something that would require a large commitment of your time, such as serving on the board of a temple or church, driving an acquaintance to a dental appointment, or watching a neighbor's pet while she goes on vacation. In these types of situations you can usually respond with, "Can I get back to you on that in a day or two?" This delay will enable you to gain composure, consider more options, and develop a calmer and more reasonable response.

University professors, high school teachers, and public speakers use delays to avoid friction with students and audience members. When a student voices a strong opinion about a topic that isn't relevant to the lesson, the teacher might say, "Let me think about what you're saying until tomorrow. I'll get back to you then." The simple delay until the next day often defuses the situation.

Avoidance by Responding Indirectly

We're amazed by how many people think they have to respond right then and there in difficult situations. With some thought, you can become very creative in finding better times and ways to handle a problem than with an immediate face-to-face response. For example, one of us found that when his children were growing up, if he discovered they had broken a rule it was sometimes better for his wife to speak to them. As the messenger she was usually calm, and she did a better job of dealing with the children in a constructive manner.

As another example, you might be able to avoid direct contact with an angry employee or co-worker by responding with a thoughtful email or with a memo or letter rather than dealing with the issue in person. This might provide a helpful time delay and you might then express your thoughts about the conflict in a less angry way.

Avoidance is even possible when anger is triggered by your husband or wife. After a breakfast confrontation, you might be able to send an email from work that expresses your ideas better than if you had responded immediately. Naturally, angry, impulsive emails can also be destructive. So we recommend waiting until your anger has subsided before sending email. In fact, we routinely enlist the opinion of a trusted co-worker or friend before sending email related to emotional issues.

We don't say avoidance is a cure-all. We just want you to consider it as a basic first step because temporary avoidance will give you time to rethink your problems and, hopefully, handle them better. In some situations, avoidance might provide the best, temporary solution to the challenges you're facing. Now, consider your own life. Are there any anger triggers you could temporarily lessen by avoidance? Try to apply an avoidance strategy to one ongoing problem in your life.

Identify an ongoing problem where avoidance might be beneficial:

_____

_____

The strategy I'll use is: ___ Planned avoidance

___ Time delay

___ Responding indirectly

THE PRACTICE OF ESCAPE

Some situations just can't be avoided. You might have difficult meetings you must lead, family functions you have to attend, and baseball games or recitals that your child expects you to be at. In these situations, it's wise to think of ways to remove yourself when you begin to feel angry. These are some options you can consider.

Time-Outs

There are clearly times when it's best to walk away from disagreements. As anger gets worse, continued discussion might become unproductive and more damaging. For example, you could take a break by telling your teen child, "I'm upset now. So I'd like us to talk about something else for a while (or go out to eat, or watch TV for an hour). We can try to solve this problem later." Or when a conversation with a wife or husband or romantic partner becomes too heated, you might say, "I don't like where this is headed right now. Why don't we each take the rest of the afternoon to think and we can try to talk this out again later tonight."

When the conflict is occurring on the telephone, it's even easier to say, "We probably shouldn't continue this right now. I'll call you back tonight." Although time-outs from conflicts require thoughtful action on your part, leaving situations when your anger starts to increase might be a good way to begin developing better control.

We've found that three simple steps are useful when teaching people to effectively use time-outs. First, identify one situation where you typically become angry with someone and there's a big argument. In this initial step, practice getting away (for example, by going out for a walk to cool down) after you've made one negative statement out of anger.

After you catch yourself saying something in anger — just leave! It might take some practice for you to become aware of your reactions and to stop the angry conversation. After you've successfully done this a few times, the second step is to observe your own internal experience of anger and practice leaving situations before saying *anything* negative. As you notice your anger build, don't say anything at all — just leave! After you've been successful with this step several times, shift your focus to the third step — working on more elegant exits.

In this step, before removing yourself, tell the other person you're becoming angry, you're going to leave, and you'd like to try to resolve the issue at a later time. It's important in this last step to follow up and attempt a resolution to the problem. Practicing these three steps will break up your usual pattern of making negative comments and will give you a sense of success and better self-control.

Planned Escapes

It might be difficult to just leave some situations when your presence is expected. However, consider this: If you know in advance that dealing with someone is likely to get you angry, it would make sense to limit the time spent seeing that person. Once people become angry, they tend to spend too much time and energy on unproductive dialogue. This kind of "You said..." "No, I didn't" "Well, I heard that with my own ears" "What I meant was..." "Well, you didn't say that" is always unhelpful.

Sometimes you can schedule only brief periods of time for problem situations. You can say up front that you have time constraints. Before a difficult meeting (or telephone conversation) begins, you might say,

"I'm happy we can talk about this. But I want you to know that I only have a half hour; then I have to (see a client/make an overseas phone call/go to a school board meeting/go to the dentist, and so on)."

We're not suggesting you lie. Rather, we suggest you organize your schedule in a way that limits the length of potentially difficult situations. Your meeting *can be* scheduled before an actual dental appointment or school meeting so you *really do have to* leave after thirty minutes. Another possibility that fits the category of planned escape is to have a co-worker, friend, or family member help you get out of a situation that's likely to be unpleasant and lead to anger. For example, you might ask your assistant to interrupt a meeting after thirty minutes to remind you about your next appointment. To use this escape strategy, you'll have to anticipate situations in which you're likely to become angry and to have a plan in place to leave the situation early.

Distraction

Thinking over and over again about a problem might increase your anger and doesn't usually produce good solutions. Therefore, there's a real place for distraction. "Putting your head in the sand" for years will probably increase anger, because some problems do get worse over time. In the short term, however, it might be helpful.

"Distraction" simply means becoming absorbed in non-anger-related and — preferably — enjoyable activities. After an anger-filled workday, you might go to a bowling alley, a baseball game, a movie, or dinner with a family member, or you might have a phone conversation with an old friend. It's important that the anger-related situation *not be discussed*.

And, if anger-related thoughts intrude during a recreational activity, you'll have to work to let them pass and bring your mental focus back to the activity at hand. The goal is to break the cycle in which you obsess about the event that led to your anger. Instead, you focus on more positive thoughts and pleasurable activities.

Think about something you have to do this week that might provoke your anger but you can't avoid. See if you can apply one of the escape strategies. Or if you unexpectedly find yourself becoming angry, see if you can remove yourself gracefully from the situation. Use the box to think about this more.

Identify a situation where escape would be useful:

_____

_____

The strategy I'll use is: ___ Time out

                                   ___ Planned escape

                                   ___ Distraction

We recommend that you use avoidance and escape in the early stages of learning to control your anger — before you've had the chance to develop the new skills, or when you're at risk for getting into serious trouble because of your anger. Although they can be very useful in the short term, these strategies don't allow meaningful personal growth. Avoidance and escape are also less helpful in situations that grow worse with time. Using these strategies alone won't be enough for you to live a calmer and happier life. Ultimately, we want to help you develop new skills to manage problem people and situations and to keep your anger low. In the next chapter, we begin this process by introducing you to a well-researched skill — "social problem solving."

KEY POINTS TO REMEMBER

- Not all problem people and situations need to be confronted. Learning to recognize which situations are worth dealing with and which to let go will help you manage your life with less anger.

- Avoidance is anticipating problems and keeping away from people or situations likely to trigger your anger.

- Escape is removing yourself from situations after you notice your anger is building.

- Avoidance and escape strategies are simple first steps that you can use to break up angry behaviors that seem automatic.

- Work at using some of the avoidance or escape maneuvers in problem situations in your life. Find out if you can get better at sidestepping problems.

- Avoidance and escape strategies by themselves aren't enough. The skills presented in the following chapters are important for you to better manage your anger in the long term.

CHAPTER 5

FIND NEW SOLUTIONS TO SOCIAL PROBLEMS

There's more than one way to look at a problem, and they all might be right.

— NORMAN SCHWARZKOPF, U.S. Army general

Struggles are a part of life, and dealing with them is one way that we human beings grow. Hopefully, the struggles you face will help you become wiser and more mature. Life without difficulties and conflicts is impossible; and if it were achievable, it would cause intellectual and emotional stagnation.

Yet some people seem to believe that such a "state of bliss" — a life without hassles — is possible and even good. They get bent out of shape when unavoidable problems come up. Their vision of life, we believe, is unrealistic. True personal development is achieved by calmly looking at problems, hunting for reasonable (but often not perfect) solutions, and growing through the process of finding those solutions.

You've probably noticed that not everybody becomes wiser with age. Some people grow from misfortunes; others don't. Those who don't are often stuck in their own anger. They complain, remain unhappy, and wind up being rejected by others.

Your reactions to the struggles, both big and small, of life have consequences. If you look at problems as challenges to be met and if you minimize anger while working on those challenges, it's likely that you'll have satisfying results. Learning how to react constructively to difficult people and situations requires personal awareness and a willingness to explore new approaches. If you scream and yell, pout and throw things, and close your mind to suggestions, it's unlikely that there will be desirable results. In a lot of ways, how you approach problems sets the stage for your life to improve, get worse, or stay the same. People who develop wisdom remain relatively unflustered, remember lessons from their past, and use those lessons to anticipate which responses to future problems will bring about good results — and which won't.

One of the downsides of anger is that people tend to get caught up in it. As a result, they don't pay attention to the most basic question: "Is what I'm doing working? Is it effective? Am I getting what I want?" Consider these different life situations:

> *Marriage:* What happens when I yell at my wife? Does she feel better? Do I feel better? Do we grow closer? What can I do to actually solve our problem?

> *Work:* What happens when I argue with my co-workers? Am I seen as an effective employee? Does our work improve? What could I do to resolve our conflict and create a better and more productive workplace?

> *Driving:* What happens when I curse at other drivers on the road and tailgate them? Do they become better drivers?

> *Parenting:* What happens when I yell, "No!" as my children are nagging me? Do they feel better? Do I feel better? Do we grow closer? How can I help them get what they want, while keeping them safe and creating a minimum of discomfort for myself?

In our professional work, we've met a lot of people who weren't aware of the consequences of their actions. They faced problems by obsessing about what they saw as unfair and unjust. They complained and whined about everyday as well as unusual frustrations. They contemplated and fantasized about revenge. They pouted and shouted. They used a variety of harmful avoidance activities like drinking, excessive gambling, and substance use. They stayed away from their homes, from school, and from their family members for long periods of time. Obviously, such reactions don't lead to successful problem solving.

We think you have a choice. How you react to difficulties over the long term will affect the quality of your life, and we want to help you achieve the best, most satisfying life possible. We hope you'll be able both to reduce your anger and to develop more constructive solutions to the challenges you face.

SOCIAL PROBLEM SOLVING STYLES

You've probably developed a consistent approach to the way you face difficulties. Over time, this approach has become a pattern that's part of your personality. Psychologists Dr. Thomas D'Zurilla and Dr. Arthur Nezu have found that most people have one of three social problem solving styles — two of them negative, one of them positive. Which one do *you* use to tackle difficulties?

Negative Problem Solving

People who use negative problem solving see life's challenges as threatening and overwhelming. They have little confidence in their ability to find solutions. They doubt their skills. They say such things to themselves as "It's too hard. There's nothing I can do. This problem can't be solved. There's just no answer." Their pessimistic viewpoint limits their search for solutions, and their results are likely to be bad.

Negative problem solving is broken down into two styles: an "impulsive, careless" style and an "avoidant" style. Both are bad, as shown in the boxes that describe the stories of Mark and Marjorie. Mark's way of dealing with misfortunes illustrates the "impulsive, careless" style of problem solving. The "avoidant" style of problem solving is illustrated by Marjorie's pattern of inactions. If you use either of these two styles, changing the pattern is very important.

As we said in the previous chapter, it's often wise to temporarily avoid problem situations or people to minimize anger. Knowing which situations to avoid and which ones to face is a key issue in negotiating life. In the story of Mark, no harm would likely come from deciding to ignore and avoid rude drivers. In fact, his life would improve. However, in Marjorie's story, not facing her ongoing work and family problems resulted in worse consequences and a lot of personal emotional distress.

We hope that our position about avoidance is clear by now. Avoidance is acceptable in the short term but is a bad long-term strategy for dealing with important life issues. Over time, avoidance makes difficulties compound, often leading to more frustration, anger, and worry.

Mark: The Road Rager

Mark, a thirty-two-year-old carpenter, had strong anger reactions that caused problems for most of his adult life. A particular area of concern was anger while driving. He would speed up, tailgate, and yell obscenities at drivers who cut him off or who drove too slowly. He did this impulsively, without thinking about the possible results. In one serious incident, he followed a car that had cut him off until he pushed it off the road. Both cars stopped safely on the grass. Mark jumped out to tell the other driver off. However, as he approached the other car, that driver took out a gun and threatened Mark. Although the incident shook Mark, he didn't change his behavior. In fact, he was arrested several times for reckless driving and eventually lost his license. Mark always said he regretted these incidents, but they continued since he drove for months without a license. In the heat of the moment, he rarely considered his options for dealing with rude drivers. For him there was only one thing to do — confront!

Mark had similar difficulties at work. Although he had a good work ethic, he was unable to handle disagreements with other workers and with customers. Minor criticisms from other employees or supervisors led Mark to respond impulsively with long angry speeches, criticisms of the other person, and occasional pushing matches. If a customer complained about his work, without thinking about the criticism, he immediately labeled the person as "picky, spoiled, and impossible to please." Also, he sometimes intentionally acted carelessly and damaged property. His anger-driven, impulsive pattern of reacting showed itself

almost every day. Over time, his reactions damaged his personal relationships, derailed his career, and created a host of additional frustrations for him.

Marjorie: The Avoider

Marjorie was an outgoing and bright thirty-eight-year-old woman who worked as a counselor for a not-for-profit agency. She was recently divorced and had two young children, ages six and eight. Marjorie had a good deal of financial stress, which in part led to an ongoing struggle with her ex-husband, who didn't pay the agreed-upon child support. She was also having difficulties at work. Marjorie didn't get along with her immediate supervisor and was overlooked for promotions that she thought she deserved.

On the surface, it appeared that Marjorie possessed the personal strengths to cope with life's pressures. However, Marjorie rarely faced problems directly. Typically, she avoided seeing people when it might lead to conflict, with the hope that things would take care of themselves. For example, instead of looking for another job, she waited in silence, hoping that her supervisor would leave. Instead of hiring a lawyer to get child support, as her parents and friends advised, she put it off, hoping that her ex-husband would comply on his own.

Because of her lack of action, her difficulties simply got worse. And as her problems intensified and built up she found herself increasingly overwhelmed. Over time, her life became chaotic. When questioned about what she would do, Marjorie said simply, "Lots of people are in situations like mine. I doubt there's any real solution." Feelings of anger, bitterness, and sadness dominated her daily life.

Positive Problem Solving

At the other end of the spectrum are people who see life's problems as challenges to be met. They're generally optimistic, patient, and committed to getting the results they want. They have a thoughtful, careful approach to life and make decisions that aren't ruled by anger. Look at Bernie, for example.

It's easy to see how the social problem solving patterns of Mark, Marjorie, and Bernie had different effects on their lives. If you're like Mark or Marjorie, the good news is that with effort you can change the way you make decisions and respond to the unavoidable hassles of life.

Bernie: The Problem Solver

Bernie was a cheerful, outgoing, and intelligent car sales representative. Over the course of his life, he had his share of difficulties and struggles. He married his high school sweetheart at age twenty-four. They were very happy. Unfortunately, when he was in his early thirties, his first wife died unexpectedly, leaving him with three children to care for. Within three years, he remarried a woman from work. This marriage failed and ended in divorce but also produced a fourth child. During his working years, he spent most of his income providing for his children. He also had the usual ups and downs that go along with child rearing, managing a household, and advancing his career.

By his fifties, Bernie had developed a style of grace under pressure. When faced with a difficulty, he had a certain childlike curiosity about trying to find the one solution that would provide the best results. He chose mostly to not react immediately or emotionally to problems. Instead, he would temporarily step back. This often allowed him to put his energy into some simple information gathering at the library, searching the Internet, or asking trusted friends how they might approach a situation. Bernie was always in a state of learning and growth. Each struggle brought about a new opportunity to develop skills and knowledge. He usually found a creative way to navigate a challenge, and he almost never made difficult situations worse. His four children graduated from high school with good grades and went to local universities. One is now an accountant, one is a teacher, another a stay-at-home mom, and the fourth followed Bernie's career path and works in the automobile industry. Because of his approach to problems, over the years Bernie became someone others frequently sought out for advice.

We can't give you advice on how to tackle the specific problems you're facing. You know your struggles best, and you're ultimately responsible for your choices. Rather, in this chapter we teach you about a technique known as "social problem solving," in which you come up with a menu of options, pick the best one from that menu, and learn and grow as you make your choices. Let's begin.

STEPS FOR SOCIAL PROBLEM SOLVING

Step 1: Clearly identify the situation and come up with potential solutions.

The first step is to identify a problem that you're facing. In chapter 2, we labeled these "anger triggers." To identify the trigger in a clear and objective fashion, we recommend using a "when-then" format. This format helps you be concrete and specific.

The "when-then" begins by focusing on the problem. It then flows to understanding your personal reaction. Let's work through an example by considering Billy, who was having frequent arguments with his wife. When he first came for counseling, Billy was fuming. He said, "My wife, I think she's crazy. All she does is yell; and naturally I yell back. She acts this way all of the time. I don't know what to do. Damn!" He kept on like this for quite a while, not giving any detailed examples. So we asked Billy to describe a specific time when they had an argument. He said, "It happened just two nights ago. I came home late and she went into one of her fits. She yelled. I yelled. Finally I just said, 'Drop dead!' and I left."

Seeing how unproductive this was, we said, "Billy, please describe what happened in one sentence. Put this sentence in a 'when-then' format. For the 'when,' tell us what you did. For the 'then,' tell us how she reacted." With some coaching in how to outline his problem, Billy finally said, "**When** I came home late from work last night, my wife (**then**) became angry because I didn't call to tell her I would be late, and the situation (**then**) turned into a serious argument."

By using the "when-then" format there's less excess, descriptive baggage, such as casting blame or magnifying the situation. Also, it's important to make sure that only one problem at a time is identified. Each problem you're interested in will require a new starting point.

Although putting your problem into this format isn't always easy, with some thought it can always be done. For example, let's assume your problem is that your ex-husband continues to call, harass, and argue with you. Identifying the problem as "I want my ex-husband to stop calling" isn't specific enough to work with. Instead, reformulate the problem as "**When** my ex-husband calls and says rude things, **then** we argue and **then** I think it will never be over and I feel lousy for the rest of the day."

Once the trigger (**when**) and the outcome (**then**) is clearly identified, the next step is to come up with multiple solutions. By multiple solutions, we mean several options, reactions, or paths that are available to you as you attempt to deal with the problem. Now, let's return to the example of Billy. The question for him to ask is "What could I do to avoid an argument the next time I come home late?"

See how many potential solutions you can develop for Billy's situation. Don't stop at the first or most obvious one. The goal is to develop a *range* of potential solutions. Part of the social problem solving approach is to think about problems differently and to identify possible courses of action you wouldn't normally consider. At first, you might find yourself going to an extreme solution. That often happens and is perfectly normal. For example, "**When** I come home late and my wife gets angry at me, **then** I could tell her that she doesn't understand the pressure that I'm under and that she should shut up, or I could ignore her and just go to bed."

When angry, people often think in narrow and distorted ways. However, once you begin to imagine all the alternatives that are available, it becomes easier to see more effective solutions. You might come up with some solutions that upon reflection seem bad or are likely to make your problems worse. If that happens, just continue to force yourself to think of other possibilities. With persistence, you'll eventually come up with several constructive alternatives. Also, we want to point out that with practice the whole process becomes easier.

Notice, that the two options proposed above (tell her to "shut up" or ignore her) are *extremes*. One represents direct confrontation and the other avoidance. When angry, it's common for people to have difficulty thinking of "middle ground" alternatives such as explaining, discussing, and developing a mutually agreed-upon plan for how to behave when someone gets home late.

So when generating potential solutions, you want to develop a list that includes a full range of actions — from ineffective to effective. How many potential solutions you identify will depend on the problem, how creative you are, and how much you practice. We recommend you come up with at least five reactions to a problem. If you can come up with more, that's even better.

Now, back to our example of Billy. He has put the problem as "**When** I come home late and my wife gets angry at me, I **then**...." What could he say or do? See if you can come up with at least five alternative responses. A sample Social Problem Solving Worksheet for this example is provided at the end of this chapter. You can jump ahead and look in the alternative responses column to see if your solutions are similar to Billy's.

Step 2: Assess the probable outcomes of each response.

The next step is to evaluate each action in terms of the outcome that it might produce. What would actually happen both in the short term and long term if Billy pursued that specific course of action? Your job is to take some time, ask yourself questions, and imagine how events would likely unfold. Outcomes are written next to each alternative until each item on the list has been explored.

Short-term outcomes are the immediate reactions you're likely to get from others. However, we want you to be alert at this point. Focusing only on immediate outcomes can be a mistake. For example, being angry and harshly yelling at your child for fighting with her sister might result in immediate compliance. Thus, at first it seems like a good alternative. However, over the long term, harshly yelling at your child will likely create emotional distance in your relationship and model bad behavior for him or her to follow.

Long-term outcomes are those that unfold over time. The effects can last for hours, days, months, or even years. For example, hitting someone or causing property damage to "teach them a lesson" might feel good in the moment. However, in the long term it might result in problems with the law that could be time consuming, disruptive, and costly.

Usually, you can judge what will happen if you take a particular course of action. Sometimes it might be less clear, and you'll have to just go with your best guess as to what might happen. Again, the goal is to come up with the most likely result. As you evaluate outcomes related to each action, don't prematurely rule any actions in or out until you've gone through your entire list.

Now, back to Billy. Jump ahead and take a look at the short- and long-term outcomes listed for the five proposed responses on the Social Problem Solving Worksheet at the end of this chapter.

Step 3: Select the best alternative and put it into practice.

The next step is to choose the alternative that might be best. You can first eliminate choices that are unlikely to lead to a desirable outcome. In our example, responses 1, 2, and 3 ("Tell her I'm stressed and hungry and I'm not going to talk about it," "Avoid her. Stay out late. Go drinking," and "Tell her she's just like her mother") aren't likely to be effective. Responses 4 and 5 ("Stop and get her flowers" and "Apologize and ask what to do in the future.") might be worthwhile. They're likely to reduce the conflict in the short run and strengthen the relationship over time. Usually, there are two or three choices that might produce a good outcome, and the real task is picking among those options. In this example, the last alternative will likely produce the best solution for the long run.

Select the best option

A short word about apologies is in order here. This social problem solving model is aimed at finding the best long-term solution to conflicts and challenges. Often it requires that you say something to the other person. In the example of Billy, response 5 suggests that he begin with an apology.

Apologies are often difficult, especially when some anger is involved. If you sense that you've been mistreated, neglected, or otherwise harmed, you might ask, "Why should I apologize? I didn't do anything wrong. It's my friend (or wife, husband, child, boss, or cousin) who should apologize." We certainly understand this position. When you're angry, there's usually some moral indignation about who is "right" and who is "wrong." Nevertheless, an apology will often set the stage for resolving the problem. For example, if Billy thinks he was truly wrong for coming home late and not calling first, he might say, "I want to apologize for my behavior. I was wrong and I'm sorry. I'll try to behave better in the future."

However, there are a lot of situations in which you don't think you were wrong and you think it would be silly to accept all the blame. In those situations, you might focus on the larger problem. For example, you might say, "I'm sorry that our relationship has reached this point. Although I don't like what you did, I understand that I also played a part in what happened. I'm sorry about the whole thing and hope that we can move forward and find a solution." This specific response might not fit your exact situation. But you get the point. Beginning with some statement of regret, no matter how mild, can go a long way toward making a solution work.

As you work toward selecting the best solution, evaluate the skill needed for any specific course of action. A common mistake is to choose a solution that will produce the most positive outcome but that you might not be able to complete successfully. Be realistic.

For example, we worked with Ronald, a cook who was unhappy about his salary. Directly asking his boss for a raise while agreeing to take on more responsibility seemed to be the best option at first. However, the strategy was risky because he didn't possess the skills to create a better food menu nor to respond to criticisms from his boss about his performance. It turned out that a more realistic option was for him to update his resume and see if other employers would offer more money. In his situation, taking time to develop the skills necessary to successfully negotiate a raise might also have been a good long-term solution. Ronald could receive coaching about how to respond to his boss' potential criticisms. With practice, he might be able to develop skills to help him ask his boss for a raise. Ronald would also have benefited from reading about assertiveness. You'll do this in chapter 10.

Step 4: Implement and evaluate.

Once you've decided on a course of action — and you believe you have the skills necessary for it — the final steps are (1) implementation: carry out the planned response; and (2) evaluation: observe what happens.

As we stated at the beginning of this chapter, greater awareness of how your reactions influence others contributes to your overall growth and effectiveness. When you're starting to learn to solve problems differently, it can be helpful to work with a trusted friend, family member, or counselor. In our personal lives we, too, consult friends about difficult problems before we choose a course of action.

Putting It into Practice

To help you put the social problem solving strategy into practice, make several copies of the blank Social Problem Solving Worksheet provided at the end of this chapter. Pick a specific current problem you're facing, and put it into the "when-then" format. Come up with alternative responses and list them on the worksheet. Imagine both the short-term and the long-term outcomes and list those for each alternative. Then, select the alternative that's likely to bring about the most desirable result. Execute the plan and observe what happens. If you've found a trusted friend, family member, or co-worker, discuss the whole issue with that person. Use this model on one or two problems each week until the process becomes more automatic.

CONCLUSION

Social problem solving gives you a thoughtful plan of options for dealing with problems. In the universe of anger management techniques, we've found it to be among the most practical because it can be used in a wide range of situations. It's likely you can apply this simple and very effective four-step procedure to a range of situations to help you deal with anger. The key is to open your mind and allow yourself to think about problems in a different way. This will lead to more effective behaviors and, very often, long-term solutions.

In the next chapter, we focus on changing the thoughts that create a lot of your anger. The techniques we present there blend well with social problem solving.

KEY POINTS TO REMEMBER

- How you approach social problems sets the stage for conditions in your life to improve, get worse, or stay the same.

- Indicators of negative social problem solving include impulsive decision making, angry responses, avoiding, and hoping that problems will resolve themselves.

- Positive social problem solving is characterized by an optimistic, patient, careful approach to facing difficulties. It includes seeing problems as challenges to be faced.

- Social problem solving steps include (1) outlining the problem in concrete terms, (2) generating a menu of options, (3) picking the best course of action from that menu, and (4) learning and growing as you make your choices.

- The simple four-step approach can be applied to a wide range of situations and can help you find constructive solutions to the problems you face.

- Make copies of the Social Problem Solving Worksheet and use them to find solutions to two ongoing challenges you're facing.

- As difficulties come up in your day-to-day life, see if you can go through the social problem solving steps in your head to find reasonable (but not always perfect) solutions.

Billy's Social Problem Solving Worksheet

1. **Describe the problem (use a "when-then" format). Include what was done, what was said, and what you thought.**

   (When) Sometimes, after a hard day at work, I stop off for coffee (or a drink) with my friends.

   Yesterday, a bunch of us stopped off at the mall. I knew my wife had cooked dinner, but I forgot to call and tell her I'd be late.

   (Then) I appeared at the door. She had a frown on her face and said angrily, "Where the hell have you been? I've been waiting for an hour and now dinner is overcooked!"

   I think she didn't understand that I had major problems at work and needed to be with my friends for a while.

   I tell her so! We go back and forth, arguing and yelling. Finally, I said, "Just shut up."

   Then, I went to the basement and watched TV. She went to bed.

2. **Now, list at least five possible responses and their likely short-term and long-term outcomes.**

Possible Responses	Short-term Outcome	Long-term Outcome
1. Tell her I'm stressed out, that I'm still hungry, and that I don't have to answer to her.	We eat dinner in bitter silence.	Lack of communication. Ongoing bitterness.
2. Avoid her. Leave the house and go drinking.	She becomes very angry, then worried.	We don't talk for days. She's quietly uncooperative.
3. Tell her she's just like her mother!	More arguing. She tells me I'm selfish.	We never work this situation out.
4. Stop and get her flowers before I come home.	She's both angry and happy.	She feels temporarily better until it happens again.
5. Apologize. Ask her what to do in the future when I forget to call her.	She vents a bit, then gives me suggestions. I listen. Some sound OK, some don't.	Together, we develop a plan and agree what to do in the future.

   [Howard Kassinove, Ph.D., and Raymond Chip Tafrate, Ph.D., *Anger Management: The Complete Treatment Guidebook for Practitioners* © 2002]

Social Problem Solving Worksheet

1. **Describe the problem (use a "when-then" format). Include what was done, what was said, and what you thought.**

   When _____

   Then _____

2. **Now, list at least five possible responses and their likely short-term and long-term outcomes.**

Possible Responses	Short-term Outcome	Long-term Outcome
_____	_____	_____
_____	_____	_____
_____	_____	_____
_____	_____	_____
_____	_____	_____

   [Howard Kassinove, Ph.D., and Raymond Chip Tafrate, Ph.D., *Anger Management: The Complete Treatment Guidebook for Practitioners* © 2002]

CHAPTER 6

CHANGE THE WAY YOU THINK ABOUT YOUR LIFE

What we think, we become.

— BUDDHA, philosopher

No matter how hard you work to develop effective skills to deal with difficult situations or how hard you try to stay calm in the face of misfortunes, you can bet that life will continue to present you with new and unexpected challenges. For example, long-held jobs will be lost, illnesses will develop, happy marriages will disintegrate, children and friends will act foolishly, good intentions will be misunderstood, gossip will be spread, and teachers and supervisors will be unfair.

For this reason, it's important to develop ways of thinking realistically about misfortunes and to view them for what they are — unpleasant inconveniences. The overwhelming majority of the anger-related situations you deal with are social in nature and don't threaten your life. That's why we refer to them as "inconveniences." Most anger triggers, regardless of how horrible they seem at the moment, usually cause little more than the loss of time, dignity, or money.

In this chapter, we'd like to introduce you to six ways to think intelligently about struggle and misfortunes so that a lot of your anger can be lessened. This approach is very *simple*. At the same time, it isn't *easy*. Awareness, thoughtfulness, and practice are required on your part to learn to think differently about the difficult parts of life. The goal is to react less strongly to daily hassles and inconveniences through a shift in how you view the world.

HOW YOUR THINKING CREATES YOUR ANGER

Like all human beings, you're a thinking creature. By this we mean you constantly sense, observe, interpret, evaluate, and make judgments about your experiences — rather than just reacting to them. The way you think about events has a powerful influence over your feelings and

actions. Your thinking contributes to your anger and to some of the self-defeating behaviors that go along with it. Over time, patterns of thought develop. With years of repetition, these thoughts become automatic and inflexible.

If you're like most people, you're probably unaware of how you're thinking when anger triggers appear. After all, your thinking patterns seem perfectly normal to you because you've been using the same ones over and over again. Becoming more aware of how you typically think when you become angry and changing these long-standing thoughts are key in reducing anger. The good news is with some effort and practice you can change the way you think about unpleasant events and thereby reduce your anger and increase your joy and happiness.

You may also wrongly believe that your anger is caused by the disagreeable and unwanted behaviors of others. In chapter 3, we referred to this as the "big mistake." In reality, since you're in charge of how you think, you have more control over your anger than you realize. Consider the following example:

You're on a busy highway and you suddenly notice a driver in the left lane swerve his car to move into your lane. He doesn't seem to see you. So you hit the brakes to slow down and gently beep your horn to let the person know you're there. As the driver swerves in front of you, you notice that he honks his horn angrily at you and holds up his middle finger.

Check the boxes below next to those thoughts that would lead to little or no anger in this situation.

☐ (1) This guy is an ass and deserves to be taught a lesson.

☐ (2) I don't know anything about this person. Maybe he wasn't paying attention. I'll let it go.

□ (3) Who does he think he is? I'm not going to take his crap. I'll show him that I'm not intimidated.

□ (4) I'm getting too old to react to this kind of stuff. I can stay calm and in control.

□ (5) He shouldn't be acting this way. He's being completely unfair since he's the one who wasn't paying attention.

□ (6) It would be nice if all drivers were fair and considerate but some aren't. That's just the way the world is.

□ (7) It's terrible that he's doing this. I'm not going to stand for it.

□ (8) This *isn't* a big deal. I don't have to react.

Obviously, there's a wide range of thoughts that people might have in response to this situation. As you can understand, how you think contributes greatly to the intensity of your anger and whether you'll retaliate by beeping, tailgating, etc. You probably guessed that the thoughts listed in the second, fourth, sixth, and eighth boxes are the ones most likely to lead to the least anger.

How do people develop thinking responses like these that allow them to easily let go of their anger? We now turn to specific steps that two cognitive behavioral therapists, Dr. Albert Ellis and Dr. Aaron Beck, developed that help people reevaluate and change how they think.

Step 1: Develop awareness of, and skepticism about, your thinking.

There are two problems that make it difficult for you to change your thinking. First, most of us are unaware of our own thoughts. If you try to tune into the flow of your thoughts, in real time, you'll notice that moment by moment your mind is busy dealing with a vast amount of information. You're constantly making judgments, evaluations, and predictions about your experiences. Since your thoughts are always with you and are part of your daily existence, it's unlikely you spend much time being aware of them.

To illustrate this point, sit quietly for thirty seconds and observe what's going on in your mind. Try to be more conscious of your thoughts. Put this book down and see if you can focus just on your thoughts. You'll notice that thoughts come and go and your mind will drift.

Now, think of the last time you were angry. Can you recall what was going through your mind at that time or what you were telling yourself? Again, put this book down and give it a try.

If this is difficult, complete the following sentence:

The last time I was angry, I thought _____.

You might notice that some of your thoughts are easy to find and with minimal effort you can describe them. For example, what are you thinking right now as you read the words on this page? You can easily get to your thoughts in the here-and-now once you focus on them. Other thoughts, however, are fleeting and are below the level of your conscious awareness. For example, when you think about yourself, what do you see as your worst flaw? You can find your deeper beliefs, but it will take more effort to become aware of them. Becoming more aware of how you think and evaluate situations when you're angry is a crucial first step towards improving your life.

A second problem with changing how you think is that you, and most everybody else, take your thoughts to be "the truth." That means you're likely to have confidence in what you're thinking. You believe that you're interpreting events, others' intentions, and the world correctly and making judgments that lead to good decisions and healthy behaviors. Although they certainly seem real to you, the truth is that your thoughts are mostly a product of your own history and learning. Let's look at Louis, Daniel, Kathy, and Wayne, who are all in their early twenties.

Louis grew up with strict parents who had the attitude that children should do what they're told with no "back talk." There was also a strong sense of right and wrong, and he learned that it was important to stand up for what is right at all costs.

Daniel grew up in a household that emphasized relationships and getting along with others. He was taught that it was sometimes necessary to consider the other person's perspective, even when you think you're right.

Kathy was taught to be careful in relationships. Trust was something that others had to earn. Being independent and strong was the most important thing.

Wayne was treated harshly by his parents. Unfortunately, he developed little confidence in himself and frequently worried that he wouldn't measure up to most people's standards.

Let's assume that all four of these individuals are in the early phase of a romantic relationship. The people they're dating keep showing up forty-five minutes late for planned get-togethers. They all have thoughts about what their partner's behavior means and what they should do about it. Based on the little bit of historical information you have, see if you can match each item on the following list of thoughts with the correct person. Place the name of each person next to the thoughts below.

a. "My date isn't really that interested in me. I'm going to end things first to make a point that I'm not needy."

b. "This is bullcrap, and I'm not going to put up with the lateness any longer."

c. "It's probably my fault. I must have said something that offended this other person. I always mess these things up."

d. "I don't like what's happening and I want to find out what's behind it."

The answers are a=Kathy; b=Louis; c=Wayne; d=Daniel. It's easy to see how the different histories of these people shaped how they think about their ongoing experiences. You make a lot of evaluations about events in your everyday life and, to some extent, your evaluations are guided by your previous experiences.

At this point, we ask you simply to recognize that your thoughts might not be accurate, realistic, or even helpful. This may be especially true at those times when you experience anger. So as you read further, please do so with an open mind and some skepticism about your thinking.

In sum, the first steps in starting to get a handle on how you think are to (1) become more aware of your thinking, and (2) be willing to see your thoughts as a fleeting private stream of words that are influenced by your personal history and might or might not reflect truth.

Step 2: Identify what you think when you feel angry.

In chapter 2, you were introduced to the anger episode model and the Anger Episode Record. Perhaps you've already filled out a few of the anger records. If not, go back and make a copy of the form on page 40 and complete the Triggers and Evaluations sections. Examine several anger experiences, and see if you can pinpoint the thinking styles that are most common for you. You'll notice that you're limited to choosing from six specific thought categories. These are labeled as follows:

Awfulizing (example: At the time, I thought this was one of the worst things that could be happening.)

Low frustration tolerance (example: I thought I couldn't handle or deal with this situation.)

Demandingness (example: I thought the other person should have acted differently.)

Negative global ratings of others (example: I thought the other person was "bad/worthless/a real #@*%&," etc.)

Negative global ratings of self (example: Deep down, I thought I was less important or worthwhile.)

Distortion (example: My thinking became messed up; I didn't see things clearly.)

There are probably a lot of types of thoughts that go through your mind when you experience anger. These six are important because they contribute to anger development. Dealing with them will do a lot to help you manage your reactions better in the future. So even though it might at first seem awkward, see how much of your thinking fits with them. Although these beliefs were described in some detail in chapter 2, we'll now review the reasons why psychologists consider them to be problems.

Awfulizing has to do with exaggerating the consequences or the level of hardship associated with difficult situations. Perhaps you describe hassles using words such as "awful," "horrible," or "terrible" rather than simply "unfortunate," "bad," or "inconvenient." This is a problem because "awful," "terrible," and "horrible" are very strong words. If examined carefully, they mean that *everything has been lost.* These words are most on target when describing the massive devastation due to earthquakes, airplane disasters, tornados, hurricanes, or when it's life itself that's lost. However, when these words are used to describe everyday frustrations, setbacks, and hassles, they exaggerate the negative. They're too strong to accurately describe what is taking place.

Describing your everyday challenges as "awful," "horrible," or "terrible" reduces your motivation to skillfully face misfortunes. It also interferes with coming up with effective solutions to problems.

Low frustration tolerance is the tendency to underestimate your ability to deal with discomfort or misfortunes. When difficult or unfair situations come up, the question often is "Can it be tolerated?" It's actually pretty amazing how often people use words that suggest an inability to deal with problems. You might say, "I can't stand it" when waiting in a long, slow-moving line; "I'm at my wits end" when a child spills juice on the rug after being warned to be careful; "I can't deal with this crap anymore" when an expected promotion falls through; or  similar words for a variety of setbacks and irritations. Seeing misfortunes from the perspective that "I can't deal with it" will increase your anger. Even more of a problem than awfulizing, it will also distract you from coming up with effective solutions. Additionally, whining and moaning about your inability to tolerate or cope with unpleasant events makes you less pleasant to be around.

The fact is that life is full of challenges, both big and small, and the real meaning of "can't stand it" is "I'm going to die." In reality, most people who are betrayed, lose their jobs, fail in school, are rejected, and so on, *do* stand it; that is, they eventually adjust and adapt. Life moves forward whether or not you think you can cope. So why not be optimistic, or at least realistic, about your skills and abilities?

Demandingness is taking how you want others to behave, and how you'd like the world to be, and making these "wants" into unbendable rules. These rules are then imposed on yourself, on others, and on the world. By being demanding, you forget that the world is complex. Conditions won't always be arranged so you get everything you want. People will often act in ways you dislike.

The bad behavior of others is determined by a variety of factors, such as human nature, imitation, learning history, and cultural norms. Your personal demandingness ignores reality, imposes rules on others, and leads to trouble. Demandingness is reflected in terms such as "must," "should," or "has to." These terms suggest no alternative.

Now, some things in this world "must" happen. We agree that we must eat, sleep, breathe, etc. There's absolutely no choice with regard to these behaviors. But, even if you're very bright, must you go to college? Must your boss appreciate your work? Must your husband do what you ask? Must your children listen to your advice? Must your teachers recognize your hard work? Must your students realize how hard you worked on today's lesson plan? Must the gardener or electrician arrive when expected? Must that new computer work perfectly when you get it home? Must other drivers be courteous? The reality is that even under the best of circumstances you'll experience a lot of disappointments. People will act in ways you don't like or expect.

Is it wise to always insist that other people conform to your terms? We think not! Is it possible to give up your demands to control people and situations and still live a joyful life? We think yes!

Negative, global ratings of others is the strong tendency to overgeneralize about people. You condemn the person as a whole for one thing he or she does. As part of this blame, you use inflammatory language such as "dope," "SOB," "idiot," and "moron." Have you ever called that slow driver who won't let you pass "an ass?" Have you referred to a telephone salesperson as "a real jerk?" By doing so, you're rating that whole person, not just what he or she's done or said. The problem with this type of thinking is that, in actuality, all of us do a lot of good things and some bad things. Some people do more bad deeds than others, but even those people do some good deeds once in a while. That slow driver might be going to volunteer in a school, and that telephone salesperson might be trying to earn some extra money for the community ambulance corps.

Every person you know and love will occasionally act in a way that's disappointing. What is the best way to think in these situations? Across work, family, social, and romantic areas of your life, labeling people harshly when they do something you dislike will interfere with your ability to preserve relationships and maintain the connections that enrich your life.

Negative, global ratings of self is exactly the same pattern described above except you direct your evaluations at yourself. You might blame or condemn yourself when things don't go well. At those times, you might criticize yourself harshly. You might say, "I'm a loser," "I can't do anything right," or "I'll never succeed." This thought pattern leads to sadness, guilt, and more anger, and reduces your motivation to fix the problem. Global self-ratings take time away from focusing on the specific problem and interfere with your ability to come up with realistic solutions.

Distortions are incorrect conclusions about the motives, intentions, and behaviors of friends, family members, co-workers, and others. At times, you might see the actions of other people as intentionally offensive. Vishal, a forty-one-year-old midlevel manager in a large corporation, felt anger toward his supervisor. He viewed his supervisor's abrupt manner as evidence of disinterest and dislike. However, a closer look revealed that the supervisor acted this way with everybody. The supervisor himself was under great stress. His abrupt manner was related to his own difficulties and had little to do with his ideas about his employees. When you distort and misinterpret the motivations of others, you don't consider alternative explanations about their behavior.

As you track a few of your anger episodes using the Anger Episode Record from chapter 2, see which beliefs are on target for you. Keep in mind that thoughts most immediately connected to your anger experiences are the ones of interest. Psychologists call this a "self-monitoring task." We're asking you to keep track of your thoughts and to become more aware of them.

Step 3: Think differently in anger situations.

Each of the six beliefs that underlie anger has a rational alternative. These rational thoughts will allow you to evaluate difficult situations in a more flexible, reasonable manner. Look at the Evaluations section of your Anger Episode Records and see which belief (awfulizing; low frustration tolerance; demandingness; negative global ratings of others; negative global ratings of self; or distortion) comes up most often during your anger experiences. If there are several that occur frequently, pick one to work on for the practice exercises that follow.

Replacing awfulizing with moderate evaluations. If awfulizing is your most common belief, you might benefit from learning to label hassles in a more moderate manner. Usually, "inconvenient," "unfortunate," "bad," or "difficult" are better descriptions of the troubles you face. These terms aren't meant to minimize the seriousness of the struggles that you experience or the discomfort you have. No one wants to be rejected or hurt; no one wants to lose money, a job, or prestige. Rather, the words are offered as more realistic descriptions. Below, we present some examples of how to make changes in this pattern.

Awfulizing Beliefs	Rational Alternative Beliefs
It's *terrible* that my boss treats me unfairly and doesn't recognize the good work I do.	Although I *don't like* the way my boss treats me, there are far worse work situations to be in.
It's *horrible* that my kids keep fighting with each other.	The constant bickering between the kids is *unpleasant.*
It's *awful* that my boyfriend broke up with me.	The way this relationship ended was really *bad.*

Now come up with two of your own statements that reflect awfulizing. See if you can change the way you think by developing more moderate language to describe your experiences.

My Awfulizing Beliefs	My Rational Alternative Beliefs
It's *terrible* (or *awful* or *horrible*) that...	
It's *terrible* (or *awful* or *horrible*) that...	

Increasing frustration tolerance. If low frustration tolerance emerged as a common theme for you, it's important that you see life's difficulties as manageable instead of continually telling yourself you can't handle them. When a problem comes up, it's OK to say you truly don't like it and wish it didn't happen. However, it will be less useful to say you can't stand or deal with it. Describing triggers as difficult and frustrating will serve you better than whining and moaning about how you can't cope with them.

The following examples show you how to think differently about your struggles.

Low Frustration Tolerance Beliefs	Rational Alternative Beliefs
I *can't stand it* when my wife criticizes me.	I *can* listen calmly to my wife's complaints. I'm a mature person who is able to hear other people's perspectives.
I *can't deal with* Bob's obnoxious behavior.	Some people will never learn to be considerate. I *can handle* hearing Bob's comments, and I don't have to take all of them seriously.
I *can't take* my kid's crying anymore.	Babies cry a lot. That's part of being a parent. I don't have to get angry, and I *can stand* hearing it.

Write in a few of your own statements related to low frustration tolerance. Try to come up with new statements that emphasize your ability to cope with problems.

My Low Frustration Tolerance Beliefs	My Rational Alternative Beliefs
I *can't stand* (*deal with, cope,* or *take*) . . .	
I *can't stand* (*deal with, cope,* or *take*) . . .	

Giving up demands and becoming more flexible. Demandingness is a common thought in most anger experiences. Changes in this area will require you to replace words like "must," "should," or "has to" with language that's less rigid. For example, it's perfectly acceptable for you to say that you'd *like* your boss to treat you with respect. However, it's very different to say that your boss *must* treat you with respect. It's OK to say you *want* things to be different but less helpful to *insist* that they be different. To be clear, let's look at some examples below.

Demanding Beliefs	Rational Alternative Beliefs
James *should* tell the truth.	It would *be better* for everyone if James was honest about what happened. However, there's no guarantee that he'll be truthful.
The office manager *must* respect my seniority.	I *want* the office manager to respect my seniority.
Debbie *should* show up on time for her appointments.	It would be *more considerate* of Debbie to be on time. But she's one of those people who always seems to be running late.

Now, come up with a few you noticed in your own thinking. See if you can make the switch to a less rigid and more flexible stance.

My Demanding Beliefs	My Rational Alternative Beliefs
_____ *must* (*should*, *has to*) ...	
_____ *must* (*should*, *has to*) ...	

Replacing negative labels with acceptance. It's easy to make exaggerated judgments about others when they do things you dislike. Changing this pattern requires that you replace negative labels ("jerk," "dope," "ass," and so on) with more precise descriptions of people's specific behaviors. It's still OK to view some behaviors of others as bad, but refrain from making global judgments about those people. Take a look at the examples on the next page to see how this change can be made.

Negative Global Ratings of Others	Rational Alternative Beliefs
Rick is such a *jerk* because he argued with me in public.	There are a lot of times when Rick is thoughtful and well meaning. However, *one quality* that I don't like about him is that he sometimes says nasty things about me in front of others.
The office manager is a *real moron*. What a *fool* (or *jerk*) she is!	Even though the office manager made this nasty decision, she's *treated me well at other times.*
Austen is a little *monster*. He never listens to the rules.	Austen is *still very young* and has a lot to learn. I hope his parents can help him to be better behaved.

Find a few examples of when you labeled others harshly. Try to change this labeling to a description of the behaviors, rather than condemning the whole person.

My Negative Global Ratings of Others	My Rational Alternative Beliefs
_____ is such a *jerk* (*fool, moron, idiot*).	
_____ is such a *jerk* (*fool, moron, idiot*).	

Accepting your own fallibility. If labeling yourself harshly when you make mistakes, have setbacks, or act in a careless manner is common for you, then you can benefit from becoming more accepting of your behaviors. Again, this will require that you replace harsh labels of yourself as a total person with descriptions that portray your behaviors in a less extreme way. The examples we present show you how to make this change.

Negative Global Ratings of Self	Rational Alternative Beliefs
I can't believe that I messed up the job interview. *I'm such a jerk.*	*I wasn't well prepared* for that interview. Next time I'll be ready.
I'm such an *idiot* for forgetting the appointment.	*I forgot the appointment.* Sometimes, I do things like that. I'll see if I can reschedule.
I'm a *horrible* person for treating Adriana that way.	*I made a mistake* when I treated Adriana like that. Next time I'm in this type of situation, I'll handle it better.

Now, come up with a few examples of when you were hard on yourself. See if you can shift to a less extreme evaluation of your faults.

My Negative Global Ratings of Self	My Rational Alternative Beliefs
I'm such a *jerk* (*fool/failure/ imbecile/idiot*) because . . .	
I'm such a *jerk* (*fool/failure/ imbecile/idiot*) because . . .	

Reducing distortions and being more accurate when interpreting the unwanted behavior of others. To change this pattern, you'll have to resist the urge to jump to conclusions about why others' behavior is crummy and to consider alternative explanations. Consider the facts and evidence related to the situation, and come up with a better interpretation. If you don't know the facts, suspend your judgment until you have more information. Here are some examples.

Distorted Beliefs	Rational Alternative Beliefs
Because my supervisor doesn't listen to my ideas and is always in a rush, *he doesn't think my work is any good.*	My supervisor seems to always be in a rush and to never listen to anyone. It might be that he's under a lot of pressure, and *it has nothing to do with my performance.*

Distorted Beliefs *(Cont'd.)*	Rational Alternative Beliefs *(Cont'd.)*
Eileen canceled our date at the last minute. She said something came up. *It probably means she isn't interested.* Women are such jerks.	I don't really know why Eileen canceled. *Maybe something serious happened.* I'll call her in a couple of days to see if she wants to get together.
Derek keeps interrupting me when I speak. *He doesn't respect me.*	I've noticed that Derek isn't a very good listener. *He seems to interrupt people a lot.*

Come up with a few examples when you jumped to negative conclusions about the actions of another person. See if you can create some alternate interpretations that fit well with the information about the situation.

My Distorted Beliefs	My Rational Alternative Beliefs
_____ acted this way because...	
_____ acted this way because...	

Step 4: Practice new thinking in your day-to-day life.

Making a real change requires you practice the new thinking patterns in day-to-day life. Also, we've found that most people change their views rather slowly. Although it will take some time, it will definitely help if you practice these better thinking patterns aloud. Don't be afraid to say to your wife, "I now realize that I really can tolerate my boss's behavior. It's silly to whine about what a jerk he is. I'm going to learn to take his actions in stride." We ask you to apply these new ways of thinking over the next few weeks. See how it feels. See if it helps.

One simple way to do this is to pick one of the six thought categories that's on target for you. Pick one to focus on as you go about your day. Change just that one thought. This means saying the new thought to yourself when you're faced with difficulties. Then, find a trusted friend you can say it aloud to. Once you feel confident that the new way of thinking is becoming more automatic, try another one.

The goal of this chapter is for you to give up imprecise and exaggerated thinking, and to accept the reality that unfair situations are part of life and that it's very possible to tolerate most unfair events for very long periods of time. Such events might be truly and strongly unlikable — but they're tolerable. Thus, we encourage you to develop a less demanding and more tolerant outlook on the struggles you face so that you'll experience less anger. In chapter 9, you'll return once again to the topic of thinking and you'll be asked to go through several types of intensive practice and rehearsal to make some of these new thinking patterns more automatic.

The thinking styles we covered in this chapter will help you develop a perspective to deal with typical adversities such as rejections or family discord. What about those truly difficult situations that happened in the past and are of major proportions? In those cases, a shift in thinking style might also help. Sometimes, however, only forgiveness can free you of your anger and distress. We cover the very important topic of forgiveness in the next chapter.

KEY POINTS TO REMEMBER

- Your thoughts are products of your own history and learning; therefore, your thinking isn't the gospel truth and might not always be accurate, realistic, or helpful.

- Pinpoint which of the six irrational thinking patterns are common for you during your anger episodes.

- Replace awfulizing with more moderate evaluations.

- Change statements that reinforce low frustration tolerance with statements that emphasize your ability to cope with problems.

- Give up demands in favor of more accepting statements about the behavior of others.

- Refrain from highly negative global evaluations of other people. Instead, describe their specific behaviors.

- Replace harsh evaluations of yourself with statements that reflect acceptance and a willingness to learn from mistakes.

- Resist the urge to jump to negative conclusions about the actions of others, and consider alternative explanations.

- Practice new thinking patterns in your day-to-day life until they become more automatic. When possible, practice aloud.

CHAPTER 7

FORGIVENESS

The stupid neither forgive nor forget; the naive forgive and forget; the wise forgive but do not forget.

— THOMAS S. SZASZ, psychiatrist and academic

We agree that life is filled with all kinds of problems, disappointments, and conflicts. As we noted in the previous chapter, most of these events don't meet a real definition of awful or terrible. Some events that have led to your anger, however, might have been of truly major proportions. You might have been the victim of an assault, a terrorist action, or religious, sexual, or racial oppression. Perhaps you, a friend, or a family member was physically abused, beaten, or maimed.

These events can lead to anger that lasts a lifetime. That kind of anger often goes along with an intense desire for justice and revenge. You might feel bitter. You might think over and over again about the event. And you might be unable to move forward with your life. If you've been the victim of any of these kinds of incidents, we offer our sympathies and wishes for better times in the future.

If your personal anger has developed after problems with your children, wife or husband, or friends, you might be able to use many of our seven proven techniques to improve your relationships with these people. Sometimes, however, in spite of reasonable efforts, it's impossible to work toward solving the problem. The person who harmed you and you're angry with might be unwilling or unable to meet with you to work on the problem. That person might have moved far away, might be in jail, might have a mental illness, or might have died. On occasion, as when something of great value has been stolen in a robbery when you weren't at home, the offender might be unknown.

We recall Fred, a thirty-one-year-old student who was angry at a girlfriend who unexpectedly rejected him. He was bitter for years afterward, even though he now had a happy marriage, two children, and a good job. His former girlfriend had no interest in talking to him about what happened years earlier. Then there was Marie, whose father worked long hours when she was young. He was basically an absentee parent as he tried to provide for his family. At age forty-three, she was still angry at him for not attending her piano recitals and sporting events when she was a child. Now, at age seventy-one, her father had developed Alzheimer's disease and talking to him about her disappointment and anger was of little use.

Whether your own anger trigger was of major or of minor significance, a basic question is this: Can the problem be remedied? If so, move in that direction with the techniques we present in this book. If not, it might be time to simply forgive and move on with life. After all, the goal is always to reduce *your* anger, which is likely to be harmful to *you* in the long run.

Forgiveness interventions are related to the thinking strategies presented in the previous chapter. Those strategies focus on seeing situations logically and accepting the realities of life. Forgiveness moves even further by emphasizing perspective taking and letting go. This approach is useful for minor (as when a child spills a drink on the floor), moderate (as when an ex-wife repeatedly doesn't listen to your ideas), and major (as in robbery and assaults) anger triggers. With some thoughtful analysis, you can learn to let go of the past, move forward, and live a calmer and happier life.

WHY FORGIVENESS IS IMPORTANT

What happens if you're not forgiving? Well, you might spend time recalling and rehearsing past adversities and harboring grudges. You might have thoughts of blame and fantasies of revenge. These thoughts lead you to remain in the role of a victim, since *you* continue to focus on how someone else hurt you. Since your emotional energy is focused on the past, you remain powerless.

Not forgiving goes along with continued anger. The mental rehearsal and grudge holding about past events leads to self-defeating behaviors and high levels of emotional arousal and can contribute to serious medical problems such as heart disease and stroke. Over time, the continued anger and failure to achieve resolution takes a physical and emotional toll on your body. Certainly, we recognize that adapting to mistreatment at the hands of others isn't easy. Nevertheless, realistic adaptation, coupled with letting go, is often required to improve life over the long term. Forgiveness is one way to adapt.

Unforgiving Responses

Later in this chapter, we'll outline specific steps you can take to develop a forgiving response to disappointment, misfortunes, or harm you experienced in the past. However, let's begin by defining the opposite — unforgiving responses.

There are a lot of ways to be unforgiving. Below, we review some common reactions we've seen over the years. These represent unsuccessful strategies that people have used to cope with unfairness and misfortunes. Regrettably, these strategies tie up emotional energy and interfere with the ability to create and experience joy and happiness. As you read further, see if they apply to you.

When you're unforgiving, you probably mentally rehearse or "ruminate," thinking over and over again about the situation or person that led you to become angry. Images and thoughts might enter your awareness, even if they're unwanted. You might imagine what the other person said as well as other details about the event and how you felt at the time. You might mentally review how unfair the situation was and think about how the other person intended to harm you.

Another symptom of not forgiving is holding grudges. Nearly everyone has held a grudge at one time or another. Perhaps someone seriously disappointed you and you continued to harbor resentment. We know of thirty-eight-year-old Perry and thirty-six-year-old Todd, brothers who got into an angry argument when Perry's wife didn't attend a family funeral. Todd decided that she was "stupid and intolerable," and he refused to speak to Perry and his wife for ten years. The grudge holding altered behavior between their family members and negatively affected their parents, children, and sisters and brothers. Family gatherings and holidays became awkward events since people had to pick sides.

Grudge holding can also occur in relation to minor everyday social situations. For example, Marion, age thirty-four, once said, "Why should I take Veronica (age nine) for ice cream now? Last week, when I asked her to clean her room, she paid no attention to me. This isn't the first time, and it's gone on for too long." Marion forgot that young children don't remember these things from one day to the next. Taking her daughter for ice cream would be a bonding experience and isn't realistically related to what happened a week earlier.

Grudges suggest a desire to show power, to dole out retribution, and to retaliate. Actually, grudges do little good, are often the result of unrealistic thinking and bad decision making, and result in negative effects for the people involved. If you continue to hold grudges, improvement will be difficult.

Avoidance also goes along with not forgiving. Avoidance can take a lot of forms and might be part of long-term anger reactions. You might avoid people or places connected to a past anger event. After going through a difficult divorce, for example, forty-three-year-old Alex now avoids social gatherings where his ex-wife's friends might show up. He said, "Some of them might be taking her side and I don't need them!" Unfortunately, Alex lives in a small town. His avoidance limits his social life. He avoids almost anyone connected with his ex-wife and has never learned whether seeing them would be as bad as he thinks (such situations often turn out to be better than people realize). His continued anger and avoidance limit his growth and ability to move forward from the divorce.

As we mentioned in chapter 1, another form of avoidance is using alcohol or other drugs to deal with anger. Some people use substances to escape from negative thoughts and uncomfortable sensations. These interfere with your ability to put the past in its proper perspective and to move forward. Using alcohol and drugs to deal with anger is a high-cost strategy that is likely to lead to a lot of other problems.

The most serious and dramatic characteristic of an unforgiving response to misfortune is the desire to seek revenge. This appears in many ways. For some people revenge takes place only in their minds and is limited to fantasy. We've met many people who have spent a lot of time and energy thinking about how to "get back" at acquaintances, family members, co-workers, strangers, and others who they think have harmed them. Perhaps that's you. Do you think about how you might "tell him off" or "let her have it" if given the opportunity to safely do it? Or maybe you think of ways to create difficulties for someone else or consider plans that would make the other person suffer.

Some people write multiple drafts of letters or emails expressing their anger, hoping to come up with words that will hurt their target. Even this type of rehearsal wastes time and energy. And when direct confrontations occur or letters actually are sent, they rarely cause the offending person to suffer as much as is wanted. This is because those who have led us to become angry have their own view about the situation that makes sense to them.

For other people, angry and vengeful thoughts play out in ways that don't involve actual confrontation. Common examples include gossiping, refusing to cooperate, minimally cooperating, secretly damaging property, and sabotaging business deals. You might, for instance, decide that you're not going to cooperate with your wife's request to attend her mother's birthday party because you're angry about an argument you had last month. Even if you do attend, you might remain distant and unfriendly.

Revenge fantasies set the stage for more serious aggressive actions. Just turn on the nightly news to see the most current examples (a gang member retaliates to "even the score," a high school student who felt misunderstood shoots his classmates, an employee who lost her job returns to murder her boss — just to name a few). Revenge takes a serious toll on human life and leads to a great deal of misery and suffering.

Religion and Forgiveness

Philosophical and religious thinking have traditionally encouraged forgiveness. Religious leaders who preach tolerance, love, and acceptance have recommended it. In fact, all major religions advise forgiveness although they differ in how it is to be approached. No matter what your own faith — or nonfaith — we hope you'll find it useful to briefly review with us what Christianity, Judaism, and Islam say about forgiveness. Following the review, we'll describe our own, science-based approach.

The Christian position is shown in biblical quotations such as "Father, forgive them; for they don't know what they do" (Luke 23:34) and "For if you forgive men their trespasses, your heavenly Father also will forgive you; but if you do not forgive men their trespasses neither will your Father forgive your trespasses" (Matthew 6:14,15). The idea that seeking revenge isn't the right course of action guides Christian forgiveness. Rather, the goal is to allow God to take care of the situation in a fair and just manner.

Even if the offender isn't willing to repent, the goal is to forgive. This idea is shown in Romans 12:19, which states, "Dear friends, never avenge yourselves. Leave that to God. For it is written, 'I'll take vengeance; I'll repay those who deserve it,' says the Lord." In Christian forgiveness the idea is to recognize that offenders require forgiveness, that forgiving the offender is your choice, that God will eventually fix the problem, and that when you're struggling with forgiving it's useful to pray and talk with someone you respect and trust such as a pastor or friend.

The Jewish perspective is somewhat different and recognizes several forms of forgiveness. As noted by Rabbi David R. Blumenthal, a professor of Judaic studies at Emory University, "the most basic kind of forgiveness is 'forgoing the other's indebtedness' (*mechilá*). If the offender...is sincere in his or her repentance, the offended person...should forgo the debt of the offender, relinquish his or her claim against the offender. This is not a reconciliation of heart or an embracing of the offender; it is simply reaching the conclusion that the offender no longer owes me anything for whatever it was that he or she did. *Mechilá* is like a pardon granted to a criminal by the modern state. The crime remains; only the debt is forgiven."

In Judaism, the offended person isn't under an obligation to forgive. Rather, the offender is supposed to be sincere and, if possible, is to have planned or have taken real steps to correct the wrongdoing. This type of forgiveness comes with the expectation that the wrongdoer is repentant. For example, an adult woman whose father abused her is expected to grant this type of forgiveness only if the father has stopped the abuse, reformed his character, admitted his problems, and asked for forgiveness. She's morally required to forgive him only if she thinks he's sincere.

A second kind of forgiveness (*selichá*) is considered deeper. It asks for understanding of the offender's life and the development of a conception of why that person acted badly. If this kind of forgiveness is carried out, it leads to empathy for the offending person but not necessarily reconciliation. This type of forgiveness comes from reaching the conclusion that the offender, like all of us, is both human and frail. As you'll see, this is similar to what we propose below.

The third kind of forgiveness in Judaism is atonement or purification. This is an absolute and total wiping away of the anger that was instigated by the offender's nasty intentions and bad behaviors. For Jews, only God grants this type of forgiveness, as one human can't totally purify another.

Forgiveness is also central to Islamic beliefs. The Koran praises forgiveness, which is defined as overlooking the offenses of a person who has done harm by insulting you, committing physical aggression against you, or damaging your property. Again, the role of revenge is considered and it's seen as desirable to grant forgiveness even if the power to get even exists. Muslims recognize that refraining from vengeance is difficult. Nevertheless, they consider it a desirable goal that's made easier with the help of Allah.

Dr. Muzzamil Siddiqi, a former president of the Islamic Society of North America, has noted that although it's important to believe in the mercy and the forgiveness of Allah, Muslims are also directed to base their personal, human relations on forgiveness. Reflecting on how central it is, he wrote, "Forgiving each other, even forgiving one's enemies is one of the most important Islamic teachings."

These kinds of religious teachings have traditionally been the basis of how people think about forgiveness. Forgiving is central not only to Christianity, Judaism, and Islam but also to Buddhism, Taoism, and other schools of spirituality. If you find that reading religious books such as the Bible, the Talmud, or the Koran is helpful then continue along that path. However, if you've been angry for a long time, you've likely found that forgiving isn't easy. In our experience, most people require something more than reading religious books or listening to sermons to produce forgiveness. We see forgiving as requiring thoughtfulness and understanding, as well as practicing specific behaviors that demonstrate forgiveness. For that reason, we developed our science-based forgiveness process. You can use it to let go of the past and live a happier, anger-free life.

THE PROCESS OF FORGIVING

Forgiveness isn't immediate. It isn't like flipping a light switch. Rather, it occurs over time. It involves a slow mental shift that allows you to understand the person who offended you — even in the face of the wrong that was done. Forgiving leads to lowered physical arousal, a calmer body, and the ability to make better decisions and be more effective in everyday life. Forgiving involves minimizing the frequency, intensity, and duration of your anger, resentment, and thoughts of revenge.

It might surprise you to learn that forgiving sometimes involves generosity or a good deed that's offered to the person who harmed you. Unexpectedly, you might even give attention and time that contributes to the improvement of the other person's life. If the individual who triggered your anger is your child or family member, that probably makes sense. If the person is a stranger, it might be harder to understand.

Here is the real surprise: By minimizing your anger, resentment, bitterness, and desire for revenge and by offering help to the person who wronged you, you become stronger and more able to live with greater joy and happiness. In sum, forgiveness involves letting go of negative attitudes and anger and adopting a perspective of understanding, compassion, and good will toward the person who triggered your anger.

How to Forgive

Our five-stage model of forgiving consists of (1) uncovering anger, (2) deciding to forgive, (3) defining forgiveness, (4) understanding why others behave badly, and (5) giving something of value to the wrongdoer.

Step 1: Uncover anger.

The first step is to develop a full awareness of your specific anger-triggering event and a complete understanding of the anger that you've been experiencing. You might have thoughts and feelings of hate, hostility, and bitterness. And as we noted, you might want some sort of revenge. Yet, you still might not have a full and deep understanding of what happened. By talking to trusted and supportive friends or family members or by writing about the experience in a journal, you can increase your understanding of what exactly happened and appreciate the depth of your anger.

The important point is to discuss the event and not avoid your feelings — although it might be best not to act on them; just acknowledge them. You'll find that as your anger experience is brought into the open, it becomes easier to reconstruct and reevaluate what happened. Lowered angry reactions can then begin to develop.

The forgiveness process begins with the recognition that a true injustice has been inflicted. You've experienced psychological suffering and possibly physical pain, and the effects of the rejection, neglect, or harm have been truly negative. The trigger that led to your anger might have been minor, moderate, or severe. Perhaps a good friend revealed your personal secrets. Maybe you lost money to an unscrupulous stockbroker or were the victim of some other financial scam. Perhaps you were the target of major anger triggers, such as racism, sexism, or ageism that led you to lose a job or an opportunity for advancement. Or you might have been physically attacked, sexually assaulted, or otherwise injured greatly. In each case, you would be expected to experience anger, perhaps with great intensity, and your view of the world as a good place might have markedly changed.

Step 2: Decide to forgive.

In this step, we ask you to realize that continuing to focus on the triggering event ("Well, Renata did actually spread nasty rumors about me! I know it's true!") and the inflammatory thoughts ("I can't work with her anymore. I can't stand her. She's crazy.") will only lead to greater and unnecessary anger and personal distress. With this information in hand, we hope that you'll entertain the idea of forgiveness as a strategy to improve your life. We hope that you'll begin to let go of that past insult or problem, without forgetting about it.

Ask yourself some basic questions about your future.

- What might happen to my anger if those thoughts of revenge disappeared?

- If I decide to make a direct and conscious decision to forgive, what benefits might I achieve?

- How much time and effort does it take to keep the anger going and does it really help me?

- Is it possible that with less anger I'd sleep better, eat better, have improved relationships with family members or friends, do better in school, or advance more quickly on the job?

Keep in mind, no one likes being with an angry person. Although your anger began as a legitimate response to an injustice, it won't lead to improved relationships with others. No matter what the cause of your anger, no matter how called for it was, or is, it's likely to become toxic. We ask you to look at the facts, reevaluate what's going on, and consider making the decision to change.

Step 3: Define forgiveness.

Often, forgiveness seems foreign and unacceptable. After all, why forgive someone who lied to, stole from, rejected, neglected, or hurt you? We've discovered that a lot of people have difficulty with forgiveness because they don't understand what it means.

Forgiveness is a process that allows you to untangle the relationship among your thoughts, your actions, and the responses of your body. As you'll see from what we present below, *forgiving* people for what they did doesn't mean *forgetting* what they did. It also doesn't mean accepting it, excusing it, defending it, or being neutral about their nasty actions. It doesn't mean becoming passive and taking no action to make things better. Rather, forgiving requires developing a better understanding about the actions of others and taking steps to improve your family life, work life, and overall happiness.

Forgiving means letting go of the anger. It means being able to think about what happened without an increase in your heart rate or blood pressure, without sweating, without taking a drink or a drug, and without thinking about revenge. Once you've forgiven someone you were angry with, the triggering event becomes just one part of your life — rather than a central or defining part of it. Having been ignored, gossiped about, abused, mistreated by a friend, fired from a job, assaulted, or rejected by a lover becomes just one event in your very much more complex life. The event might always be central in your memory, but it no longer defines who you are. To help you make sense of forgiveness, we want to distinguish it from related ideas.

Forgetting. Most commonly, forgiving is confused with forgetting. Consider Saria, whose cousin raped her more than twenty years ago when Saria was growing up in India. She's never forgotten what her cousin did; in fact, the memories of the event linger to this day. Forgiveness, however, has allowed her to change her focus. Instead of obsessively recalling the event and thinking about how much she wants her cousin to be punished, Saria has memories of her cousin that are both of the good times they shared when they were younger *and* of his offensive, aggressive behavior to her.

Memories of the rape, as one event in a much larger relationship with the cousin, are less frequent now. When she does think of what happened and when she talks about it to others, she's relatively calm. Although she no longer sees him, Saria truly hopes that her cousin has grown up to become a happy man, that he's learned to respect women, and that he's changed his impulsive, aggressive habits. Nevertheless, Saria has never forgotten what happened.

Accepting. The word "accepting" suggests indifference and a lack of motivation to change the bad parts of the world around us. However, forgiveness doesn't mean passive acceptance. If you were wrongly hurt, it isn't proper to simply accept it. Forgiveness allows the angry person to work toward changing family, friends, or others to improve relationships.

For example, good teachers certainly know that some students cheat on examinations. Forgiving those students for their bad actions doesn't mean that cheating has to be accepted as unavoidable. Instead, good educators work to change classroom conditions to minimize the probability that those students will cheat in the future. The good educator doesn't just angrily stew about it — "Those damn kids will do everything in their power to get good grades!" — or passively forget about it — "What can I do? Kids have been cheating forever." Instead, the good educator thinks to the future: "What can I do to increase moral behavior and honesty in my students?"

In the same way, forgiving a child who sets fires or who assaults other children in the neighborhood doesn't mean we become indifferent to those behaviors. Even after forgiving, it remains important to help the child act properly to the best of our ability.

Excusing. The word "excusing" suggests that what happened was OK, as long as there was a reason for it. It also suggests treating the negative outcome as less serious than it really is. Clara, a forty-one-year-old mother of two, used to say, "So my husband drinks and yells at the kids. I think drinking runs in his family. His father did the same thing, and his brother drinks every weekend. There are worse things in the world. At least he works and provides money for the family. It's not that bad."

Well, we think it's bad! Children are most likely to thrive if they've been brought up in loving, supportive homes. It would be better if Clara's husband didn't drink excessively and if he didn't yell at his children. If Clara were to forgive her husband, she would stop making excuses for him as she attempts to cope with the situation. Although we would like her to forgive him, for the sake of her own happiness, we also want Clara and her husband to seek realistic solutions for the drinking and yelling.

Neutrality. The word "neutrality" suggests that no sides are to be taken in conflicts. However, if you're angry because of the actions of a bully, tyrant, terrorist, or other evildoer, we do expect you to take a side. The offender's harmful actions that led you to suffer might lead to problems for others in the future. Even when trying to develop a forgiving response, it's sometimes necessary to speak out and take actions so you and others aren't hurt in the future.

For example, Darin's stepfather sexually abused him when he was a young child. As he became an adult, he slowly began to let go of his anger, forgive the man, and even tolerate his presence at family functions. However, once he and his brothers, sisters, and cousins had their own families, he became concerned that his stepfather might repeat the same behavior with other children. He decided to privately share his painful experiences with some family members in order to protect their children.

Whether we're talking about injustice or discrimination in the workplace, aggression by a teenage child, or the oppressive behaviors of dictators, strong actions might be required to fix such situations. Sides are to be taken, as neutrality might lead others to suffer. At the same time, it's possible to forgive so you don't continue to suffer with personal anger based on what happened to you in the past.

Justifying. Consider forty-year-old Francine, who was married to Cole. They just had their second child and were having a hard time making ends meet. Cole was a manager in a local hardware store and already worked long hours. He often left the house at 8:00 AM and didn't come home until 9:00 PM. Because of their financial stress, Cole decided to work as a handyman on Sundays to bring in extra cash. This meant that he had to advertise, give estimates, and do the required work. He was now working seven days a week. Without rest, he became argumentative, demanding, and abusive to Francine.

She justified Cole's behavior by saying, "It's all of the hard work and fatigue that makes him do it. He really loves me. It's not the real Cole that I'm seeing these days." Although we wanted Francine to understand what was happening and to forgive Cole, forgiving didn't mean sitting back and justifying what he was doing. In civilized society, there's no justification for downright nasty acts.

Calming down. Have you ever said to an agitated person, "Just calm down?" Does it work? A simple command rarely changes human reactions. Imagine if you began to eat a salad and we said to you, "OK, look at your plate and become very angry" or "OK, think of this salad and feel guilty." It's unlikely that you'd feel much anger or guilt. That's because the development of anger and guilt requires a genuine trigger. Emotions don't develop on command.

Neither does forgiveness; rather, it's a process. It isn't as simple as someone saying to you, "Just calm down and forgive him" or "I know what she did was nasty, but just let it go." Consider Henry, who hired a moving company for his journey from New Haven, Connecticut, to central New Jersey. They agreed on a price of $2,000 for all of the work. The moving company seemed reputable and advertised that they had insurance for any damages that might occur. The move was timely and seemed to go smoothly.

Unfortunately, after he paid the bill, Henry discovered that his $3,000 large screen TV was damaged. He filed a claim with the moving company and expected a reasonable response. They, however, said it was probably broken before the move and accused Henry of trying to cheat them. Henry was furious and had a number of shouting matches with them. He wasn't sleeping well and had headaches. For him, forgiving meant reducing his anger and thinking more rationally about a better way to handle the situation. Henry hired a lawyer to sue to the company for the $3,000. He told the story to his lawyer in a calm and subdued manner. This doesn't mean the event meant less to Henry. Rather, he had put it in perspective and was now going to let the legal process proceed.

Becoming calm is very useful, but it isn't synonymous with forgiving. Part of forgiving, in this case, is an awareness of the fact that conflicts exist in life and that we have a legal process to resolve some disputes. Henry doesn't have to agree with, accept, be neutral about, or justify the moving company's behavior. Rather, forgiveness means letting go, reducing agitation, changing thinking, and, in this case, allowing others to resolve the dispute in a fair manner.

Seeking justice and compensation. We're impressed with what Gandhi said, "If we practice an eye for an eye and a tooth for a tooth, soon the whole world will be blind and toothless." Seeking justice and compensation places focus on the idea that an angry person will feel good only when some sort of revenge is taken. We met with fifty-seven-year-old Walley, whose son was murdered by an unemployed drug addict seeking money to buy heroin. The police quickly found and arrested the drug addict. At the trial, the district attorney told Walley, "I know that you're hurting and that what happened was a tragedy. You'll see that you'll feel much better once we get this thug behind bars." As expected, the murderer was tried and sentenced to a long prison term. However, Walley felt no better. His son was still gone.

We've heard this kind of story many times. Justice and compensation, even financial compensation, don't make things much better. Consider those times where people died after years of cigarette smoking and their families sued the tobacco companies. The financial settlements, sometimes for large amounts, didn't bring the loved one back. When it's all over, there's still grief. We're certainly not taking the side of the tobacco companies, who lied to the public for many years. Rather, we're pointing out that financial compensation doesn't fix the situation.

True forgiveness doesn't demand compensation. It's an act of understanding — and sometimes mercy — that hopefully will lead to less anger and distress for the person originally harmed. Also, since forgiveness is a long-term process, improved and more positive feelings might wax and wane. Justice and financial compensation and the temporary good feelings they produce don't bring back a loved one killed by a drunk driver, a friend who died in the collapse of the World Trade Center towers, a soldier killed in Iraq, a student killed in the massacre at the Virginia Institute of Technology, or someone who died in the collapse of the Interstate 35W bridge in Minneapolis.

Forgiving means something much more than feeling good and being compensated. In many situations, as when a person has been cheated of life savings, was forced to become a child soldier and kill others, or was wrongly incarcerated, there's no adequate compensation for the wrongs done. Something more personal is necessary to move forward with life. Letting go of anger, bitterness, and fantasies of revenge doesn't mean giving up the desire to make life better. The perpetrator, who you're angry with, is still accountable for the offensive act. But although there might or might not be justice as part of legal or other proceedings, you have to be in charge of your anger. No matter what happens, you'll be better off and healthier if you have less personal bitterness.

Condemning. Finally, we note that forgiveness doesn't come from condemnation. The condemning person has the attitude of "She's a totally uncaring jerk who deserves to know how much she hurt me." This attitude reflects a feeling of moral superiority, which is absent in true forgiving.

In our years of life and professional practice, we've learned the obvious: We all live in glass houses. The verse "Let he who is without sin, cast the first stone" (John 8:7) ends a well-known biblical story that's worth a review. The story goes that a woman caught in the act of adultery was brought to Jesus Christ by the scribes (lawyers) as a test to see if he was overly liberal. Although he didn't condone her behaviors, he also didn't condemn her as a total person. Rather, he thought that the lawyers who brought the woman to him were hypocrites. Christ was supposedly the only person free of sin and, therefore, the only one who had the right to cast the first stone. He forgave her and told her to not act that way in the future.

Blame and condemnation suggest that we *can* and *do* live error-free lives and, thus, have the right to judge and punish others. Ask yourself whether you've been error free in all that you've done. Even as we write this book, we both recognize that although we've tried to live good lives and to help others, we've acted in some ways we later regretted. We hope that others haven't condemned us for being human mistake makers. We try to give others the benefit of the doubt when we observe bad behaviors, and we hope you'll consider acting the same way.

Step 4: Work to understand why others behave badly.

This step involves the development of new ways of thinking about the person who offended or hurt you. This thinking encourages understanding and compassion in you. For example, if you're angry and want to move forward with your life, it might be helpful to understand the childhood of the offender and what led to the development of her or his offensive behavior.

You can learn to put the angering event in context by understanding the pressures the person was under at the time of the nasty action. What role did drugs, alcohol, an abusive childhood, a psychiatric illness, or a brain dysfunction play in that person's life? Did hallucinations, delusions, or a specific cultural background contribute to the harmful actions? Consider these examples. In some parts of rural India, it was acceptable to kill young female children, and in the past it was perfectly acceptable to keep slaves in the southern United States. The acceptance of these cultural practices lessened over time.

For you, the challenge is to understand what it was in the offender's family, culture, religion, human nature, or environment that contributed to the bad behavior. What rule was that person taught about how to treat children, criminals, women, the elderly, etc.? How did human nature and a dysfunctional environment set the stage for the person to act so badly?

We don't want you to release the offender of responsibility. Rather, your goal is to better understand the person and the life factors that led to the offensive behavior. Without excusing, forgetting, accepting, or justifying — in order to forgive — it's useful to develop empathy and compassion toward the perpetrator whose actions led to your anger. The central goal of this step is to see the perpetrator as a whole person who acted unjustly, in part because of the forces of nature, history, and environment.

Step 5: Give.

The idea of giving something to the person who offended or angered you or doing something good for that person might seem strange. Perhaps there is a family member who you haven't seen in years because of some offensive behavior that led you to feel angry. Secretly, you might still hope the person will suffer. Perhaps you're angry at a co-worker who cheated or made accusations against you and then was promoted. You might still be harboring anger when you think of that person.

Although your anger might seem justified, at some point you have to ask yourself, "What kind of person am I, and what is my anger doing to me?" In fact, reading this book might be a sign that you're already asking yourself that question. Are you a person who wants to remain a bitter, angry victim? Do you want to continue spending your time thinking about how you were hurt and how you can get even? How can you move beyond your anger?

OK, now that you understand what forgiveness is and why the person you're angry with might have acted so badly, we ask you to consider giving "a gift" to that person. We understand that this step might seem inconceivable. Yet, by giving that person something, you move out of the role of victim and into control of yourself. You move into a role of power, since you decide what kind of gift to give, when to give it, and what to say. The gift doesn't have to be a physical object, and it doesn't have to be "gushy." In fact, the gift could be symbolic or a simple gesture of good will.

Perhaps you could send a holiday card to a lover who rejected you, expressing good wishes for the future. Maybe you could send the offending person an email expressing a wish for a good holiday season. Or you could visit a terminally ill person in the hospital who offended you, or send flowers or chocolates to the hospital.

If the person who angered you has gotten much older, you might see him or her in a debilitated state and you might then take a different view of the person. If the person has died, you might consider a gift to a charity or a cause that the person liked or supported. You get to decide what the gift will be. However, some sort of behavioral action is required on your part. Surprisingly, it's you who is best served by this kind of forgiveness and gift giving. And it's you who will feel better once peace has been made.

Putting Forgiveness into Practice

As we said earlier, forgiveness doesn't occur immediately; it's important to remember that it's a mid- to long-term process. Also, forgiving unfolds differently for each person and depends to some degree on the characteristics of the situation and the people involved. The length of time it takes to forgive will be different for everybody and every event.

We've met a number of remarkable individuals who have chosen the path of forgiveness in response to serious unfairness and tragedy. We've met other individuals who decided to hold on to their bitterness and anger. In one dramatic case, a parent who struggled to follow the steps of forgiveness came to form a relationship with the murderer of his son (an interview with this father can be found in our *Anger Management Video Program* distributed by Impact Publishers).

Our conclusion is that people who choose forgiveness move forward more positively with their lives than those who remain unforgiving and bitter. The remaining parts of this chapter touch on a few lessons learned from those who have suffered extreme hardship, tragedy, and loss.

OTHER WAYS TO ALLOW YOURSELF TO MOVE TOWARD FORGIVENESS

Some victims of severe oppression write books. For example, Primo Levi, who survived the World War II concentration camps wrote *Survival in Auschwitz*. He told his story to move toward what he called "interior liberation" and to improve his own mental health.

Some people move past anger through scholarship. Dr. Viktor Frankl, another prisoner in a Nazi concentration camp, from 1942 to 1945, developed a specialized form of psychotherapy based on recovery from angering, adverse life events through strengthening trust in the meaningfulness of life and the dignity of people. Psychologists, social workers, and counselors, who study the various forms of psychotherapy in their training, are usually introduced to Dr. Frankl's contribution, which is known as "logotherapy." His contributions to psychotherapy no doubt helped him overcome the feelings he developed due to his camp experiences.

More commonly, people write poetry or stories, create films, meet with other survivors of a needless tragedy, or simply chat via email to further their personal release from anger and vengeance. Some people set up their own Internet sites to devote attention to and explore their own unique situation. Others find it helpful to keep a simple journal in which they write about each phase of the forgiving process. This allows them to establish meaning about the event and to deepen their forgiving.

If you think it would be helpful to keep a journal, we recommend you address the following questions:

- What exactly are you angry about?
- Who is your target?
- How long have you been angry?
- What are some of the reasons to keep being angry and to seek revenge?
- How does your anger benefit you?
- What are some of the reasons to let go of the anger and still hold the offender accountable?
- How does your anger hurt you?
- What was life like for the offender while growing up?
- How might the offender have tried to deal with a bad life situation?
- What prevented the offender from doing so?
- Can the offender in some ways also be seen as a victim?
- How can you develop a forgiving, not forgetting, attitude?
- What can you do to move forward with the rest of your life?

If you decide to keep a journal, think about how you want to handle the privacy of your thoughts and writings. Everyone does this differently. Perhaps, you'll consider your journal to be secret. It might represent an opportunity to talk to yourself and to express thoughts you wouldn't want to share with others. On the other hand, you might decide to have a close friend or family member share your journal. You might see it as helpful to talk with someone about what you wrote. You might even find it's better to share it with someone who you respect but who isn't close to you. This might be a teacher, clergyperson, or professional psychologist. Each of these choices is acceptable. We think you'll find that simply considering the questions, with or without feedback, is helpful.

When you begin to embrace forgiveness, it's often useful to start small. You can actually practice forgiveness in a lot of everyday situations. Once you've accepted the idea, you'll find that a lot of opportunities exist in daily life to practice it. For example, it can be used when someone cuts you off on the road, cuts in front of you in a line, misunderstands your intentions, or criticizes your work. The next time something irritating like this occurs, try these simple steps:

- Recognize that you're having the same old angry thoughts (for example, "He's a real jerk," "She's so rude," or "I'll show him; I shouldn't be treated like that," and so forth), and try to catch yourself and put those thoughts on hold.

- Briefly try to guess what might be happening or have happened in that person's life to cause him or her to act that way.

- Silently, in your mind, wish the other person well.

- Let go of your anger and walk away.

Over time, responding with forgiveness will become easier. This will allow you to decide if a more forgiving attitude makes sense for you. Once you have some familiarity with the forgiveness approach, you might decide to apply the steps above to a more significant event from your past.

THE CHALLENGE OF FORGIVENESS

You might agree that *a lot* of people who have committed offenses can be forgiven. You might recall a child, parent, next-door neighbor, or good friend who acted badly and whom you forgave. Perhaps that person revealed a secret, told lies, stole, or was unfaithful. With time, you were able to let go of your anger.

The challenge as you move forward with life is to develop forgiveness skills for *all* people who have angered you — no matter what they've done. You might not think that serious perpetrators of evil can be forgiven. Throughout history, there have been some aggressors who have caused the deaths of millions of people, while others have committed savage acts against individuals. Is it possible to forgive violent people who have committed brutal acts?

Certainly, it would be more difficult for you to forgive if you or someone you loved had personally suffered because of their actions. But with the unavoidable passage of time, is it wise for the victims of such people to remain angry, bitter, and vengeful? What is the likely effect of continued anger on the well-being of the former victims as the months and years pass? If you were a friend of someone who suffered because of a terrorist action, a mass killing, or a serial killer, what would you recommend?

Actions to eliminate future acts of aggression and reigns of terror are surely warranted. It's important that we heed the words of many holocaust survivors, "Never again." But are perpetrators of evil eventually forgivable by their victims? What is in the best interests of the victims? What is the alternative to forgiveness? To consider these questions, we invite you to read the story that follows about Eva Kor.

FINAL THOUGHTS

Forgiveness means changing your mental, emotional, and behavioral reactions. When you forgive, you *think* in different, better ways about the life of the person who offended and angered you. You think about the forces that led that person to behave badly. Over time, you begin to *feel* less anger when the problem comes into your consciousness, and you might even *act* to help the person who offended you in some way. We hope that you'll consider forgiveness as a way of reducing your anger.

For now, we leave you with the words of Nobel Prize winner, Archbishop Desmond Tutu of South Africa. He said, "Without forgiveness, there is no future." We hope that your future will be bright.

Forgiving Dr. Mengele

Eva Mozes Kor was a Jewish woman born in Transylvania, Romania, in 1934. In 1944, the Nazis sent her and her family to the Auschwitz-Birkenau concentration camp. Because she had a twin sister, Miriam, Dr. Josef Mengele selected them to remain alive for his experiments.

Mengele usually injected one twin with poison, bacteria, or a virus. He watched to see how the disease developed and how long it took for death to occur. When the patient died, he murdered the other twin to determine the effects of the disease he had caused. Mengele experimented on approximately 1,400 pairs of twins. Although Eva and her sister were in Auschwitz for nine months, they survived and were liberated in 1945 at age ten.

After World War II ended, they went to Israel, where Eva married an American Holocaust survivor. Eva then moved to the United States and became a successful realtor in Indiana. Miriam, who remained in Israel, developed a serious kidney illness from one of Mengele's injections. Eva donated one of her own kidneys to her sister, but Miriam died in 1993.

Eventually, in her quest for personal peace, Eva began a campaign to help victims of the Holocaust learn to forgive. She moved from an embittered survivor to an advocate for healing. Eva's path to forgiveness began with a trip to Germany to meet with a German doctor, Dr. Hans Münch, who had worked with Mengele in Auschwitz. Münch had been tried after World War II but was found not guilty because he hadn't actually carried out Mengele's experiments. Feeling both anger and anxiety, Eva met with and confronted him about the past. As they talked, Münch admitted he had been there during the gassings of the Jews. He said, "And that's my problem," because he suffered from depression and nightmares about his concentration camp days. After their meeting, she sent Dr. Münch a letter indicating that she forgave him.

Eva then asked Münch to join her in January 1995 at a gathering to remember the fiftieth anniversary of the liberation of Auschwitz. The extermination camp was now a museum. In front of a group of reporters, Eva read a confession of guilt from Münch. She saw it as a statement from an eyewitness that could be used to contradict those who deny the Holocaust happened.

(Cont'd.)

Forgiving Dr. Mengele *(Continued)*

At that anniversary meeting, Eva made a surprising personal statement. She said, "In my own name, I forgive all Nazis." Eva wasn't forgetting, justifying, condoning, or passively accepting what had been done by the Nazis, or by Mengele, to her or to the thousands of others who suffered in Auschwitz. Rather, it was her way of letting go of her personal hurt and emotional pain and moving on.

Some concentration camp survivors were shocked. They believed their anger was too deep to forgive. Eva, however, saw her behavior as personal and believed she did the right thing. She said, "I felt as though an incredibly heavy weight of suffering had been lifted...I never thought I could be so strong." Eva found that because she was able to forgive the Nazis, she was able to free herself from her status as a victim. Eva clarified the difference between forgiving and forgetting when she said, "What the victims do does not change what happened." She believed that all victims have the independent right to heal in their own way. "And the best thing about the remedy of forgiveness," she said, "is that there are no side effects. And everybody can afford it."

In 2006, Eva Mozes Kor's story was made into a documentary titled *Forgiving Dr. Mengele.* First Run Features distributes it, and it's available on DVD. We recommended it for those readers who are interested in the forgiveness process.

KEY POINTS TO REMEMBER

- At first, the concept of forgiveness might seem strange and unacceptable. Forgiving someone who has harmed or wronged you might seem impossible.

- Remaining unforgiving is associated with obsessive thoughts about the past, grudge holding, avoidance, and a desire for revenge.

- Principles of forgiveness have traditionally been based on religious philosophy.

- The advantages of forgiveness include less physical agitation, less anger, better decision making, a greater ability to enjoy the present, the capacity to move on, and living a happier life.

- The five-step model of forgiveness includes (1) uncovering anger and hurt, (2) making a decision to forgive, (3) defining what forgiveness is and isn't, (4) developing an understanding of why others acted badly, and (5) giving something, no matter how small, to those who have wronged you.

- Forgiveness takes time and unfolds differently for each person.

- Start small and practice forgiveness in everyday situations. Try it out.

CHAPTER 8

LEARN TO RELAX

*There must be quite a few things that a hot bath won't cure,
but I don't know many of them.*

— SYLVIA PLATH, American poet

Has anyone ever told you to "just relax?" The words are so simple to say. Achieving a real state of relaxation is much more difficult. In this chapter, after we help you to understand some basic issues about relaxation, we will teach ways to easily achieve it.

Relaxing can help you overcome your normal and automatic tendency to become angry and aggressive when you feel threatened. Notice our words "normal and automatic." In the 1900s, the physiologist Walter Cannon taught us about the "fight or flight" response. When animals of all sorts feel threatened, they have to decide whether it would be better to become aggressive and fight or to withdraw and take flight.

Let's look at some examples. A cheetah on the savannahs of Africa has killed a gazelle to feed her cubs. As they're feeding, a group of lions comes along wanting to take the food. What to do? Well, it's the anxious and smart cheetah that quickly gives up the food and takes flight with her cubs, since lions are much more powerful and can easily harm the cheetah and her cubs. If, on the other hand, elephants with calves are grazing and lions approach in a threatening manner, the elephants will show signs of an angry, aggressive fight reaction by flapping their ears, moving their heads in a threatening manner, and making grumbling or trumpeting noises. Other animals steer clear of elephants because they can do great harm to almost all other creatures.

In the animal world, staying for the fight or retreating and taking flight are natural responses that have developed over millions of years.

These responses allow the animals to avoid harm and get what they need, such as food. Even within one type of animal, there's a time for fighting and a time for fleeing. Rams, stallions, and other male animals often fight with each other for dominance and rights to the females of the group. Yet, at some point during the fight, one male gives up and takes flight, as it becomes obvious that the other is stronger.

FIGHT OR FLIGHT OR SOMETHING ELSE?

OK, you're not a lower animal. You have a different kind of brain. You can think, evaluate, and judge situations. You don't simply respond with animal instincts. That's certainly true. Yet, all of us are still partially prisoners of that old and *automatic* fight or flight reaction.

Thinking means using your brain to consider options. It means looking at situations, evaluating, and deciding on an appropriate course of action. It means considering some of the strategies for anger reduction we introduced in previous chapters, such as just leaving difficult situations, problem solving to develop new and previously unthought-of solutions, and reducing angry arousal by rethinking the meaning of situations.

In the animal world, quick and automatic fight or flight reactions are good. Such reactions can save the lives of animal young, preserve food and family members, and protect shelters. Lower animals have no choice but to react quickly because the bullying they receive from other animals is often life threatening.

In your world, however, there are two additional factors to consider. First, most of the threats you receive in daily life aren't life threatening. The most common causes of anger in the human world are insults, being misunderstood, and being ignored or treated unfairly by friends and family members. We understand that some threats, as in robbery and assault, can lead to physical harm; but most of the things you get angry about are far less urgent. Second, we have problem-resolution resources that animals can't rely on. We have rules, regulations, and laws. We can bring our disputes to teachers, friends, parents, mediators, lawyers, small claims courts, and so on. For these reasons, we're usually better off neither fighting nor fleeing. Rather, the best goal is to seek a negotiated solution that's fair and mutually beneficial.

Why Can't You Just Relax?

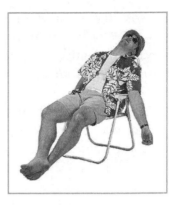

Finding a fair solution, however, takes time. You'll have to relax, take stock of the problem, rise above your natural tendency to immediately fight or flee and decide what to do. Unfortunately, simple words can't bring about the first step: relaxing. When someone simply tells you to "just relax," not much happens. More is needed than words.

PROGRESSIVE MUSCLE RELAXATION

Like the automatic fight response, the *relaxation response* is built into human nature. When it is triggered, as shown by Dr. Herbert Benson of Massachusetts General Hospital, brain chemicals are released and you'll begin to breathe slower, need less oxygen, and have lower blood pressure. Your heart rate will decrease, and you'll have fewer disruptive thoughts about your problems.

In humans, the relaxation response can be brought on in many ways. Just as exercise, an approaching aggressive dog, a viral infection, or a dentist telling you that the procedure will involve "deep drilling" on your tooth can increase your heart rate, there are various ways to bring on relaxation. No matter how you attain your relaxation response, once it's achieved, you'll be able to think more clearly and act more in keeping with your best self-interests. The relaxation response will help you react less impulsively to problems and make more positive choices. Learning relaxation techniques to remain calm in the face of provocations is an important way for you to interrupt the anger sequence.

In the 1930s, American physiologist Edmund Jacobson developed a technique known as "progressive muscle relaxation" or PMR. This is the most common, quickest, and easiest technique to use for you to develop your own relaxation response. PMR is a conscious self-control strategy that helps you relax by tensing and releasing various muscle groups. After some practice, you'll easily be able to tell when your muscles are in a state of tension and when they're relaxed.

You first learn and practice relaxation in private. Then it becomes possible for you to bring on the relaxation response while imagining stressful situations or real life anger triggers. However, we want you to understand that learning to relax is important in its own right: relaxation improves your capacity to deal with a lot of life's problems and calms your body, which has long-term health benefits. Remember, we're talking about the development of a reaction. It takes practice, and you might not achieve the deepest state of relaxation until you work on it for a while. A lot of people can do it by themselves. Some, of course, find it easier to work with a skilled professional, who can help bring it on more quickly. You may want to consult your doctor if you have pulled muscles, orthopedic conditions, or another ailment that might be affected by this activity. If you're able to do the types of physical activities that most adults can do, these procedures won't be difficult for you.

PMR is best done while sitting in a comfortable chair. A reclining armchair is ideal, although lying on a bed is OK. Find a block of time, about thirty minutes, when you won't be disturbed. Turn off your telephone, make the room semi-dark, and begin by getting as comfortable as possible. It's best if you close your eyes and, if necessary, use the toilet first. Don't wear tight clothes or shoes. Take off your eyeglasses and heavy jewelry and neckties, and don't cross your legs.

Begin by taking a few deep breaths in through your nose and out through your mouth. The idea is to get a slow rhythm going. As we describe below, what you'll be doing is alternately tensing and relaxing specific groups of muscles. After that your muscles will be more relaxed. Concentrate on the feel of the muscles, specifically the *contrast* between tension and relaxation. In time, you'll recognize any remaining tension in a specific muscle and be able to reduce that tension.

Don't tense any muscles other than the muscle group you're working on. For example, avoid the tendency to tense your arms when you're working on your legs. Stick with one muscle group while keeping the others relaxed. Don't hold your breath, grit your teeth, or squint. Breathe slowly and evenly, and think only about the tension-relaxation contrast. We recommend tensing each muscle group for about five full seconds, then relaxing for ten to fifteen seconds. During the relaxing phase, focus on letting go and relaxing your muscles even more. Each step in the process consists of two phases, a shorter, tension phase and a longer, relaxation phase.

Do the entire sequence once a day, until you're able to relax and control your muscle tension quickly. It's a good sign if you begin to sigh spontaneously.

During the relaxation procedure, it's common for other thoughts to come up and interfere with relaxation. If this happens, just bring your focus back to the sensations in your muscles and your body. If you're very tired, you might find you fall asleep. Although it can be pleasant to drift off to sleep while relaxing and this isn't a problem, remaining awake will be more helpful in the development of your relaxation skills.

Make Your Own Relaxation Tape

You can easily make your own relaxation tape by recording your voice with a tape recorder or digital voice recorder as you read the script below. Begin by giving yourself an instruction to take those deep breaths, in through the nose and out through the mouth. The rest of the procedure progresses with instructions to tense a muscle group for about five  seconds and focus on the discomfort that's created. This is what happens when you feel angry, as your muscles automatically become strained. After tensing, stop clenching the muscle, release the pressure, and focus on the warm, heavy, and relaxed feelings that naturally develop. Just let the muscles relax. Remember, tense only one specific muscle group during the tension part of the exercise, leaving the other parts of the body relaxed.

Don't go too quickly through the procedure. We repeat, *don't go too quickly through the procedure.* Slow is much better than fast when the goal is to bring on the relaxation response. We've given some approximate times for each segment in parentheses.

   START the recording here. Use these exact words.

1. OK, (use your own name), close your eyes, sit quietly for a few seconds, and focus on smooth breathing (ten seconds).

Remember, you're in control. You can regulate yourself to breathe slowly, smoothly, and deeply (wait about ten seconds).

2. Now, make fists with both of your hands and feel the tension building in your lower arms, hands, and fingers. Focus on that tension and silently describe the uncomfortable pulling sensations to yourself. That's what happens when you're angry. OK, hold the tension (five seconds). Now, release and let your hands and arms relax. Focus on the warm, heavy, relaxed feelings in your hands and notice the contrast with the tension. Just focus for a while on your relaxed hands and continue to breathe slowly, smoothly, and deeply (ten seconds).

3. Now, bend your arms, and take both of your elbows and press them firmly into your sides. While pressing your elbows inward, also flex your arm muscles. Notice the tension building up throughout your arms, shoulders, and back. Hold that tension (five seconds). OK, now release your arms, and let them fall heavily to your sides. Focus on the heavy, warm, and relaxed feelings in your arms, and continue to breathe slowly, smoothly, and deeply (ten seconds).

4. Moving to the lower legs, flex your feet by trying to point your toes toward your nose. Notice the tension spreading through your feet and ankles. Hold the tension (five seconds). OK, now release the tension in your lower legs and focus on a sense of comfort as your lower legs become more relaxed. Continue to breathe slowly, smoothly, and deeply (ten seconds).

5. Next, build tension in your upper legs by pressing both your knees together and lifting your legs off the bed or chair. Focus on the tension in your thighs and the pulling sensations in your hips. Describe those uncomfortable feelings to yourself (five seconds). Now, release the tension, and let your legs fall slowly and heavily onto the bed or chair. Focus on letting go of all the tension in your legs, arms, and shoulders. Just let go. Breathe slowly, smoothly, and deeply (ten seconds).

6. Next, pull your stomach in toward your spine. Notice the tension in your stomach (five seconds). Now, let your stomach relax. Breathe slowly, smoothly, and deeply, and focus on the

relaxation you can produce in your stomach, in your legs, and in your arms and shoulders (ten seconds).

7. Next, take in a very deep breath and hold it. Notice the tension in your expanded chest (five seconds). Now, slowly let the air out and feel the tension disappear. Notice that you can voluntarily relax your body and you can breathe slowly, rhythmically, and deeply. With each breath that you take, you can allow yourself to relax even more. Focus on relaxing and letting go of all of your tension (ten seconds).

8. Now, imagine that your shoulders are on strings and are being pulled up toward your ears. Feel the tension building in your shoulders, your upper back, and neck. Hold that tension (five seconds). OK, now just let the tension go. Allow your shoulders to droop down. Let them droop down as far as they can go. Notice the difference between the feelings of tension and relaxation (ten seconds).

9. Take your chin and pull it down and try to touch your chest. Notice the pulling and tension in the back of your neck (five seconds). Now relax. Let go of the tension in your neck. Focus on letting your neck muscles relax. Let your arms and legs relax. Breathe slowly, rhythmically, and deeply (ten seconds).

10. Now, mildly clench your teeth together and focus on the tension in your jaw. Feel the tight pulling sensation (five seconds). OK, release. Allow your mouth to drop open and relax all of the muscles around your face and jaw (ten seconds).

11. OK, now build up the tension in your forehead by forcing yourself to frown. Try to pull your eyebrows toward each other. Focus on the tension in your forehead (five seconds). Now release. Smooth out all of the wrinkles and let your forehead relax (ten seconds).

12. At this point, allow your whole body to feel relaxed and heavy. Breathe deeply and rhythmically, and relax your arms, legs, stomach, shoulder, and facial muscles. (Your name), you're in control of yourself. Every time you breathe out, silently say the word "relax" to yourself and imagine that you're breathing out all of the tension in your body. Breathe in and out five times. Silently,

say the word "relax" and let all of the tension disappear. Just let go and relax. Allow yourself to quietly enjoy the pleasant relaxed feeling for the next few minutes. (Allow two minutes to go by.)

13. OK, (speak softly), now begin to think of this room. Imagine the walls and furniture. Slowly, take a final deep breath, open your eyes, and remain relaxed until you slowly get up.

STOP the recording here.

Remember, it will take a number of repetitions to get the desired effect. The best results will be achieved if you rehearse every day. As we noted above, set aside about thirty minutes at a time when you're not likely to be distracted. Regular practice will get you to the point where you can use the procedure without the tape.

TEN ALTERNATIVES TO PROGRESSIVE MUSCLE RELAXATION

PMR has been shown to be a very successful tool to produce the relaxation response. Nevertheless, you might not find it to be ideal for you. Fortunately, there are other ways to produce relaxation. Here are a few options to consider.

1. Rhythmic breathing with a sound or word

With your eyes closed, sit quietly in a comfortable position. Think about your various muscle groups, from your feet up to your face, and let them relax. Breathe in through your nose and out through your mouth. Become aware of breathing in a rhythmic fashion. As you breathe out, say the word "one" slowly and silently to yourself. Just *slowly* breathe in and then out, and say "one" to yourself. Breathe easily and naturally, repeating the word "one" with every exhale. Continue to do this for about fifteen minutes. You can open your eyes to check the time, but don't use an alarm, which might startle you. After you've finished, take a few minutes to sit quietly with your eyes closed. Then, open your eyes and remain seated for five more minutes. After five minutes, stand up and resume normal activities.

After some practice, the relaxation response is likely to emerge with little effort. Practice the technique daily. As with traditional PMR, remove tight clothing, turn off phones, and don't do the exercise right after a meal, as digestion might interfere with the development of relaxation.

2. Calming words

Some people find it helpful to choose a calming word, such as "calm" or "mellow," to say or think during a repetitive exercise such as walking, swimming, or running. Use this word in rhythm with the steps or strokes you're taking.

3. Yoga and exercise

For a lot of people, yoga brings on a feeling of relaxation. This might be due to its focus on body positioning and breathing, which distracts you from thinking about anger triggers. You can learn basic yoga skills through formal classes or from video programs. Like other relaxation methods, yoga requires consistent practice.

In addition, having some type of physical exercise routine can also have a useful effect. Common options include walking, jogging, cycling, swimming, aerobics, spinning, weight training, kickboxing, and using a treadmill. Find a type of physical activity that matches your level of fitness and that you can easily work into your schedule.

4. Simple deep breathing

Simple, slow diaphragmatic breathing exercises, without tensing the muscles, also lead to relaxation. The way you breathe while you're angry tends to be rapid and shallow. You can counteract this by practicing a breathing response that's opposite: slow and deep. To learn to breathe from your diaphragm, lie on the floor on your back. Stretch out comfortably. Place a small book over your abdomen. Make the book rise as you inhale. Lower the book gently as you exhale. It might take a few tries before you get used to the movement: breathe IN (book rises); breathe OUT (book lowers). Practice for a few minutes over the course of a few days until this type of breathing becomes natural. Once you have it down, see if you can re-create the movement when standing, when sitting, and at other times in your day-to-day life.

5. Prayer and chanting

Any form of repetitive prayer or chanting brings on the relaxation response if done often enough. Harvard Professor Herbert Benson conducted many studies on repetitive prayer and concluded that all forms evoke a relaxation response that reduces body arousal. The repetition of sounds or words is the most important part. Praying that requires verbal or muscle repetitions brings about relaxation since deep rhythmic breathing is connected with a sound, word, or phrase. A single prayer isn't enough, as it's the repetitive nature of the experience that brings on relaxation.

Remember, repetitive prayer and the resulting relaxation response is part of the history and tradition of many religions and cultures. Jews

have a form of repetitive prayer called "davening," which consists of reciting text in a soft droning manner while bowing or rocking back and forth. Thus, davening has both verbal and muscle actions. In Eastern Orthodoxy, repeating the "Jesus Prayer" can produce the relaxation response. This calls for endless repetition of the phrase "Lord Jesus Christ have mercy on me." It's recommended that this prayer be repeated for long periods of time. Some people repeat it up to 6,000 times a day, tracking the number of repetitions using a prayer rope. If you synchronize the prayer with rhythmic breathing, the relaxation response might well emerge.

In Catholicism, the Rosary is a devotion that consists of repeated sequences of the Lord's Prayer followed by the Hail Mary and the Glory Be to the Father. When repeated nine days in a row, it's called a "novena." Some forms of Protestantism and Catholicism promote use of a "centering prayer." This involves choosing and repeating a sacred word while sitting comfortably with closed eyes. When awareness of external thoughts develops, the person gently returns to the sacred word. Similar practices exist in Islam, Confucianism, Shintoism, and Taoism.

6. Mindfulness meditation

Mindfulness meditation is a specific technique that comes from Buddhist practice, and it too brings about relaxation. This type of meditation involves learning to simply observe or notice without reacting to your surroundings. For example, you might say, "I'm cooking. I'm putting oil into the frying pan. Now I put in broccoli and carrots. A carrot fell on the floor. It looks very orange against the white floor. I'm covering the pan. I feel hot. I'm opening the window." The goal is to simply notice behavior and experiences and to name or describe them *without evaluation.* No judgments of good, bad, right, wrong, lazy, weak, strong, kind, or mean are made. As we said in chapter 6, anger emerges partially from evaluations and judgments. Thus, learning to observe without evaluation can be a powerful anger eliminator.

7. Nature experiences

You might be able to achieve relaxation by taking a walk on a sandy beach and listening to the crashing waves, or going near a field or forest in the early evening where there's nothing but the sound of crickets (if such locations are available). Spending time in nature is among the most relaxing of experiences. Try to make it a part of your weekly routine.

8. Water

You might have noticed that water brings about relaxation. Take a warm bath, walk by a creek and listen to the running water, or stand by a waterfall. Hot tubs, spas, and pools can be very helpful. For most of us, it's rather hard to be angry after spending a few minutes in a bubbling, 102-degree hot tub.

9. Massage

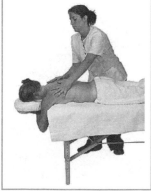

Tension and anger go along with tight muscles. It's no wonder, therefore, that a lot of people feel relaxed after they receive a professional massage. Other people don't like to have strangers work on their bodies; an electric massage chair can be a useful alternative for them.

10. Audio- and videotapes

Bookstores and Internet sites/vendors carry a wide range of relaxation-related materials. You can find helpful information on sites such as www.youtube.com and www.google.com. Just type "relaxation" or "relaxation techniques" into the search box.

FINAL COMMENTS ABOUT RELAXATION

We recommend PMR as one of the most effective means of bringing about relaxation. Nevertheless, depending on your particular interests, you might find that communing with nature, being religiously active, or other activities work better for you. Whatever method you decide to use, take the time to make it part of your routine. You'll be better prepared to make decisions about the triggers of life if you consistently practice evoking the relaxation response.

Remember, impulsive fighting and arguing or avoiding and fleeing are often our first reactions. However, angry arousal in your body can lead to a false sense of optimism and boldness that can easily backfire and cause you a lot of pain. In contrast, thoughtful and planned responding follows a relaxed body. This thoughtful reacting is likely to lead to a calmer and happier life for you.

It's useful to develop PMR so you can constructively navigate the ever-present rough waters of life. At the same time, you can use relaxation as a specific technique to reduce anger while imagining or exposing yourself to your real anger triggers. We introduce you to this possibility in the next chapter.

KEY POINTS TO REMEMBER

- Like all animals, a fight or flight reaction is part of your instinctive response to threat.

- The problem with the fight or flight response is that most of the threats you face aren't life threatening and strong physical arousal gets in the way of thoughtfully responding to problems.

- Developing the ability to calm your body and mind will help you respond less impulsively to challenging situations.

- Progressive muscle relaxation (PMR) is a technique you can use to relax. It involves alternately tensing and relaxing specific muscle groups.

- You can make your own relaxation tape with the script provided. Practice once a day.

- If PMR isn't a good fit, pick an alternate technique from the list of options.

- Take time to make relaxation part of your daily life.

CHAPTER 9

EXPOSE YOURSELF AND REACT LESS

He who angers you conquers you.

— ELIZABETH KENNY, pioneering physical therapist

Practice is necessary when learning anything such as a golf stance, a computer program, or a foreign language. Just reading or thinking about a new skill is not enough. In this chapter, we will ask you to face (in your imagination or "for real") the people, images, words, and situations that start up your anger. This is what we mean by the term "exposure."

Instead of responding to problem situations in your usual tense and angry ways, you'll be asked to learn to react with two other responses: relaxation and thinking more constructively. You're likely to react less to — and be less bothered by — the circumstances that trigger your anger if you repeatedly face these challenges thoughtfully. Having people systematically face the situations that trigger strong emotions is one way that psychologists help people overcome worry, shyness, lack of confidence in dating, and other common problems. When combined with relaxation and constructive thinking, the act of willingly and consistently facing difficult situations will lessen your anger. Before we begin, we present some cautionary notes to consider before you try exposure.

When *Not* to Use Exposure

In some circumstances exposure exercises aren't recommended. Although we can't list all of them, consider these four issues.

Lack of commitment and motivation. If you're not committed and motivated to change the way you act when you're angry, exposure might backfire. Instead of working to change your reactions, you might secretly be focused on trying to *change* the actions of others. Thus, you might be setting yourself up for increased conflict.

Active substance use. If you're using drugs or drinking alcohol regularly as a way to manage your emotions or to avoid problems, this might not be the right time to practice exposure. Your emotions and behaviors are usually less predictable when you're intoxicated or high. In addition, substance use will interfere with evaluating your reactions and will make it difficult for you to change. If substance use is a significant problem for you, read chapter 11 for suggestions on ways to handle it. Using exposure will be more helpful once your substance use is under control.

Depression or agitation. If you're prone to becoming seriously depressed or agitated, we recommend you use caution when attempting exposure. You might wish to try some of the exercises and see what effect they have on you. If you feel worse, don't proceed. If the exercises make you feel better, continue. You're the one responsible for monitoring your progress.

Uncontrollable aggression. If you have a history of assaulting others and believe that by facing people or situations that instigate your anger you might harm another person, please don't proceed. Exposure techniques might still be useful for you but are best conducted under the supervision of a trained professional.

HOW EXPOSURE WORKS

Exposure works in a number of different ways. These are some of them.

Exposure allows you to learn new skills in a realistic context. Practicing relaxation and rational thinking without actually facing your anger triggers might be pointless. It's more useful to practice these skills in situations that resemble what you typically face. As an example, look at how Doug acted when he was mad at his two sons.

Exposure leads to habituation. Human beings have a remarkable capacity to adapt and adjust to unpleasantness of all types. "Habituation" is a term that psychologists use to describe how we react to something

Doug: The Impulsive Father

Doug was a thirty-six-year-old caring father who often overreacted, screamed, and cursed when his two sons loudly argued with each other. He recognized that his outbursts of anger stopped the obnoxious behavior of his children at the moment but had little positive effect in the long term. In addition, his wife had a different view, believing that the boys' arguing and bickering was perfectly normal and to be expected. After Doug and his wife attended several counseling meetings, they agreed that although the boys' behavior was unpleasant, it was reasonably normal and not of major concern.

After examining his thoughts, Doug identified the following beliefs as part of his anger sequence: "They shouldn't be fighting and I can't stand their bickering." We taught Doug that it was his evaluation of their arguing that magnified his anger. Doug agreed that it would be a good idea to replace his irrational thought with a new one: "Bickering is common and, therefore, it's silly to demand that they not argue. I can certainly tolerate it and accept it without becoming angry." However, he found that in the real situation, when he heard his boys argue he reverted to his original thinking pattern.

To prepare himself to better accept their arguing, Doug wrote out a detailed description of a typical incident. Once he had it in writing, he imagined this scene in his mind while rehearsing the new thought. He practiced over the course of a few weeks, and the new way of thinking became more and more natural. When conflicts and arguing between his sons erupted, Doug was able to use his new thinking to calm his anger. This technique is described in more detail in the sections below.

new and how our reaction changes over time when that thing or experience is no longer new, threatening, or interesting. For example, let's say you saw a movie that was very scary and you could feel your heart beating faster and your stomach get tight. What would happen if you saw that same movie fifteen times in a row? Obviously, your emotional arousal wouldn't be the same after repeated exposures to the film; it would lose a lot of its emotional impact over time.

The same is true for some of your anger triggers. Sometimes, by just staying in a situation and taking the perspective of an observer, your anger will go down. This means giving up the desire to change the other person, make your point, or solve the problem. Certainly this is much easier said than done. If you yell or think repeatedly about revenge, you might actually be distracting yourself from the impact of what is triggering your anger. Sometimes it's wise to just observe the unfair behaviors of others without reacting. You can also learn to become an observer of your own internal reactions, that is, to describe what your anger feels like but not act on it. Over time, you'll see that you don't have to react and that your anger will decrease. The story of thirty-year-old Tina, a new faculty member in the foreign languages department at a major university, shows how exposure can work without professional intervention.

Exposure breaks short-term "reinforcement" patterns. A lot of people we've worked with say, "My anger sometimes just comes over me." If this sounds like how you see your behaviors when you're angry, they might be a function of "reinforcement"; that is, your behaviors when angry might have led to benefits that you didn't notice. As we noted in chapter 1, you've been reinforced (or rewarded) for reacting as you do and your anger now seems natural.

Tina: The Demander

Tina often became angry; seething and making strong comments when her co-workers didn't agree with her ideas about teaching innovations. Week after week she would leave the meetings in distress. Then she had a spontaneous "ah-hah experience." She realized that the university had been in existence for 200 years without ever listening to her ideas. She recognized that, although she considered her ideas to be good, there was no reason her co-workers *had* to agree with her. She also recognized that one benefit of a university job was working with others who had diverse ideas about teaching. She continued to attend the meetings regularly, and after some time, by using a good friend as a sounding board, she became much less agitated. She also began to take breaks by swimming in the university pool three times a week. By repeatedly facing the situation and not trying to change the people around her, Tina began to truly enjoy her job, and she was much less angry.

When Doug yelled, his children immediately stopped arguing. Since he got what he wanted, his strong reactions were reinforced — making it likely that he would continue his angry behavior. However, after each incident he usually felt out of control and recognized that his actions created distance between him and his sons. Doug eventually developed a new way of responding. Instead of yelling, he first took a deep breath and waited for five seconds; then, he separated his sons by placing them in different rooms and removed their computer games for the evening. In terms of stopping the fighting in the moment, this new response turned out to be just as effective as yelling. The critical benefit was apparent only by looking at the long-term results — a healthier and less volatile relationship with his children.

By thoughtfully trying different behaviors in real life situations, you can replace automatic anger reactions with new behaviors that bring about better results.

Exposure changes the way you look at things. Something else happens during the process of being exposed to negative circumstances and not acting on your anger. You learn something new about other people and the world around you. Your view of the offending person might change if you take time to understand the other person's perspective. You might learn you can actually tolerate difficult situations and don't have to react with anger.

Doug began to believe that he was a capable father who could effectively manage challenging parenting issues. With practice, he developed more confidence in his parenting skills, less intense reactions to the boys' arguments, and a better plan for shaping their behavior. Because of his willingness to face situations differently, he was able to grow.

By continuing to participate in meetings, Tina began to see her co-workers differently. She started to understand that they often had useful ideas and that they all had the same goal: to better educate the students. She began to develop more respect for her co-workers and for her own ability to deal with ideas she disagreed with.

Picking an Anger Problem

OK, now that you understand some of the basics of using exposure to deal with your anger, let's try it out. Think about some situations where you typically become angry and that generally lead to bad results. You can use the situations you identified from the Anger Episode Record you filled out in chapter 2 or think of some that have occurred more recently. List your most common anger situations in the box by providing a one-sentence description. Once you've made your list, estimate the intensity level of the anger you experience for each item by putting a rating of 0 to 100 next to each item; 0 means no anger, and 100 means the most anger you've ever experienced.

Anger Situation	Anger Intensity
_____	☐
_____	☐
_____	☐
_____	☐
_____	☐

Now, pick the problem you'd like to work on first. We recommend you start with a problem that is somewhere in the middle range of your list, one with a moderate level (between 40 and 60) of anger. The reason for not beginning with the most serious problem is that we would like you to experience some success before tackling your most difficult situations. Items with the strongest intensity ratings can be put aside until you've mastered the exposure skills presented below.

TYPES OF EXPOSURE

We'll discuss three specific exposure techniques: *in imagination, verbal,* and *in real life*. We recommend you try all three, although some will fit better with your anger situations than others. It's better to do the exposure exercises in the order they're presented in.

Exposure in Imagination

Step 1: Create an anger imagery scene.

The first step in *exposure in imagination* is to create a realistic image of the anger trigger you're facing. Remember to pick a situation from the middle range of your list. Write out a brief description of what usually happens. Include details, such as descriptions of the place, the other person, clothes people were wearing, the weather, facial expressions of the other person, tone of voice, etc. The goal is to create a scene where you can imagine yourself participating in the events and not just observing them.

As a model, consider this anger scene in which Ted argues with his wife, Jill, about money problems.

> I'm coming home after a long day at work on a bright, sunny day. I can see the yellow daffodils in the garden as I walk to the front door. The door is blue, and I notice a crack on the railing. I'm feeling relieved to be home after a hectic day.
>
> As soon as I open the door, I see Jill sitting at the table doing the bills. She's wearing her brown T-shirt, jeans, and a pair of sandals. She has an irritated look on her face and doesn't smile as I walk in. I'm thinking to myself, "Uh-oh, she looks pissed off; I bet we're going to have another fight." I feel the muscles in my back get tight and my stomach start to contract. When she sees me she says, "We have money problems again." I'm thinking, "What a bitch. She doesn't even say hello. She just starts in with me the second I get home."
>
> I try to remain calm as she continues to explain that the situation is serious and that we have to do something to decrease our loan payments. She, of course, uses a sarcastic and accusatory tone and points her finger at me. I immediately take it to mean that she's blaming me for our problems. I start to feel my face getting hot and my hands trembling. Before I can stop myself I say, "Look, this is the situation we're in; just deal with it. Maybe instead of blaming me all the time, you could pick up more hours at work."
>
> Jill gets up, puts her hands on her hips, and says, "Why are you acting so immature? You created this situation, and you're acting like a child."
>
> I stomp out of the room and go up the carpeted stairs to the bedroom. The walls are white and the bed has a light green

blanket on top of it. I sit on the bed and think of how unfairly Jill is treating me. I stay there for about twenty minutes. Part of me wants to go downstairs, have it out with Jill, and tell her how I feel. However, I know that I'll overreact and start to yell. So part of me wants to avoid her. Since I'm getting hungry, I finally go downstairs to the kitchen to make something to eat. I ask Jill if she wants anything, and she says, "No" in a biting tone. She doesn't even make eye contact with me. I'm thinking, "I'm offering to make you dinner, and you treat me like crap." I walk to the kitchen door, slam it behind me, and walk out of the house.

When writing scenes, begin with a rough draft, and then add more detail to a second version. You may feel some anger as you write the scene. This is actually desirable and indicates that the scene is on target. Once the scene is developed, you're ready to begin practice. The Imagery Scene Development Form at the end of the chapter can guide you in developing anger scenes.

Step 2: Practice relaxation in response to the anger scene.

The second step is to find a quiet and comfortable place where you're unlikely to be interrupted. Begin by practicing the progressive muscle relaxation (PMR) sequence you learned in chapter 8. Once you've completed the relaxation sequence and feel more relaxed, switch your

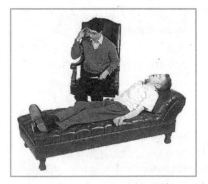

focus to the anger scene you just developed. Review, step-by-step in your imagination, the sequence of events as you wrote them earlier. Keep your eyes closed, and imagine the situation is actually happening.

Allow yourself to feel whatever anger comes up as the scene unfolds. Once the scene is finished, shift your focus back to relaxation and use it once again to reduce your tension and arousal. After this is accomplished, repeat the sequence again. A practice session might begin with relaxation followed by the anger scene and a return to relaxation. Then, the anger scene would be reviewed once or twice more, each time followed by relaxation. Begin and end each practice with relaxation.

After a number of practice sessions with the first anger scene, you'll find it increasingly difficult to feel anger. When this happens, you can move to thinking skills in step 3.

Step 3: Develop a coping statement.

Coping statements are designed to replace beliefs that increase your anger with those that help you lessen anger. To develop an effective coping statement, refer back to some of the exercises you completed in chapter 6. You'll recall you were asked to focus on six irrational, inflammatory thoughts (awfulizing; low frustration tolerance; demandingness; negative global ratings of others; negative global ratings of self; and distortion) and to identify the ones that were on target for you. You were also asked to create a series of rational alternative beliefs. If you haven't read chapter 6, do so now. If you don't remember the material, this is a good time to go back and review.

From chapter 6, pick one of the five irrational ideas that was common for you and identify the rational alternative belief you created. Look it over again and make any minor changes you think will improve it. You might have had more than one rational alternative belief. Pick the one you think is on target and likely to be the most helpful. Write it down and take a few minutes to commit this statement to memory. This will serve as your new coping statement, which you'll now practice with your anger imagery scene.

Step 4: Practice new coping statements in response to the scene.

Once again, find a quiet and comfortable location. Next, rehearse your anger imagery scene in a step-by-step fashion. Again, imagine that the situation is actually happening and allow yourself to feel any anger that emerges. As you notice yourself beginning to feel anger, stop reviewing the scene, shift your focus, and say the coping statement silently to yourself several times. Then, return to the scene where you left off. As you continue to review the situation, practice the coping statement as you notice your anger build.

Here is a brief portion of Doug's scene about his sons arguing. The points at which he rehearsed his coping statement are indicated.

> It's a rainy Saturday afternoon and everyone is inside. I hear the
> door slam with a loud thud, and then my two sons are yelling. I

think to myself, "Here we go again." (He begins to feel anger and says the rational coping statement: "Their bickering is normal and, therefore, it's silly to demand that they not argue. I can certainly tolerate it, and accept it, without becoming angry.") I hear Jeremy telling his brother to leave him alone. Sounds like they're pushing each other. Their voices are getting louder, and I think in a second I'll have to go upstairs and deal with them. (He begins to feel anger and repeats the rational coping statement: "Their bickering is normal and, therefore, it's silly to demand that they not argue. I can certainly tolerate it, and accept it, without becoming angry.")

Doug continues to work his way through his anger scene, rehearsing the coping statement at points where he feels his anger is increasing. Doug rehearsed his scene a few times, using the coping statement, until he felt little anger. We recommend you rehearse the scene with the coping statement at least twice a day, for a few days, until the statement becomes natural and automatic.

Step 5: Assess your results.

Once you've used relaxation and coping statements in response to your anger scene, you'll hopefully notice that it's more difficult to feel much anger. If this has occurred, congratulations! You're effectively facing one of your anger triggers. Before moving on to a more intense anger problem, there's a bit more practice we'd like you to try.

Verbal Barb Exposure

Most anger situations involve some sort of contact with another person. Therefore, *verbal* statements from others are likely to be common triggers for you. We call statements that trigger anger "verbal barbs." It's useful to practice not reacting to such statements. Some barbs you developed might represent what people have said when they're angry with you. Their words then trigger your anger. Doing the exercise described below will help you stay calm when you're the target of someone else's anger.

Step 1: Develop verbal barbs.

Go back and reexamine your anger scene. Think about some negative statements that another person in that situation might make to you. Think of three to five statements that would likely trigger your anger.

Also, consider the tone of voice that the other person would use. That tone might be, for example, sarcastic, threatening, angry, dismissive, or condescending. Write down those statements along with a description of the tone of voice in the spaces provided in the accompanying box. A list of example barbs that Cathleen created for a work situation with her critical supervisor follows.

Statements that my supervisor makes:	Tone of voice:
I'm sick and tired of this office being so disorganized.	Accusatory
I feel like I have to explain everything twice to you.	Angry
Not sure you have what it takes to work in this office.	Condescending
Do I have to do everything around here?	Angry

Statements that others make to you:	Tone of voice:
_____ // _____	
_____ // _____	
_____ // _____	
_____ // _____	
_____ // _____	

Now it's time to practice. Once again, you'll be using relaxation skills and coping statements. However, this time you'll use the barb statements instead of the anger scene. We recommend that you put the barb statements on audiotape or a digital voice recorder. When you record each statement, say it clearly and try to match the tone of voice in which such a barb statement would be delivered. Say the first statement and then pause thirty seconds before saying the next one. The pauses are important because they allow time to practice your relaxation skills and coping statements.

Step 2: Practice relaxation in response to the barb statements.

Play your recording, and listen to the first statement. As you hear it, focus on taking a relaxing and calming breath. Tense and release the tension from one muscle group. Resume your relaxed breathing. Wait for the next statement. When you hear the second statement, again take a relaxing and calming breath and then tense and release another muscle group. Repeat the steps of breathing and tensing and releasing until you've run through all the statements. Once you've gone through your list, do the whole thing again five more times. It won't take long. Do a series of five repetitions over the course of a few days until the barb statements no longer produce much anger. If it becomes boring to listen to the tape, you're becoming successful at hearing barb statements and not reacting.

Step 3: Practice new coping statements in response to the barbs.

Now, go back to the coping statement you used earlier with the anger scene. Listen to your recording once again. This time, however, rehearse your coping statement during the pauses. As before, run through your list five times for each practice session. Feel free to stop once the coping statements are comfortable and automatic in response to the barbs.

Step 4: Assess your results.

The idea of verbal barb exposure is for you to stay calm and use new thoughts in the face of challenging statements. If you're able to hear the statements and use relaxation and new coping statements, you're ready to move on to the next level of exposure.

Exposure in Real Life

Now that you've had some success practicing your new relaxation and coping skills in ways that are similar to real life, the next step is to intentionally place yourself in that situation. To be successful, it's important you work hard to not revert to your old angry reactions. Since you're now practiced in the skills of staying calm and relaxed and are able to understand and rehearse a new thought, the goal is to face the situation and feel minimal anger. It's important that you not react with angry statements or provocative body language or gestures. Your goal is to tolerate a negative situation and hear negative statements from others, to stay calm during them, and then to exit.

For example, we had Doug go about his usual schedule with his family and be ready to use the new skills once his sons started to fight.

Since his wife was usually the one to respond to the children when they were together, she was asked to step back in order to create more opportunity for Doug to practice his new skills. Doug was asked to take the lead in dealing with the arguing. He had to approach the boys, take a deep breath, think rationally, and solve the problem. Other examples include bringing up difficult topics with husbands or wives, revisiting rude store clerks, and sitting next to an obnoxious co-worker. Remember, the goal is always the same: to stay calm, cope and not react, and exit gracefully.

It's important to gauge your success as you take each step. If you're unsuccessful in a live practice round, carefully consider what went wrong to get you off track. If you have doubts about your ability to deal with a difficult situation, more imaginal practice might be required. If you believe that facing a particular situation in "real life" is likely to result in significant problems or a loss (for example, loss of a job when facing a critical supervisor), then skip live practice for now or think about obtaining professional guidance. Guidelines for finding additional resources are discussed in chapter 11.

Moving On to a More Difficult Anger Situation

Once you've worked through the various exposure exercises with the first problem area, you can move to one with a higher anger intensity rating. Start by creating an anger imagery scene, and go through each of the steps outlined in this chapter. Don't attempt real life exposure until you've mastered relaxation and the use of coping statements and have completed work in imagination. As new anger situations emerge in your life, you'll always have the option to use the exposure procedures with these new challenges.

A FINAL NOTE: EXPOSURE AND ASSERTIVENESS

The goal in exposure practice is to help you react less to your anger triggers and to make relaxation and rational thinking skills more automatic. Taken in isolation, this is unlikely to help you express your feelings and desires to others or make changes in your relationships. Nevertheless, once you're in greater control of your angry reactions, you'll be in a better position to deal effectively with the people in your life. To do this, it's important that you express yourself properly. Therefore, assertiveness skills are the topic of the next chapter.

KEY POINTS TO REMEMBER

- Exposure refers to facing the people, situations, and words that instigate your anger.

- When done properly, exposure leads to confidence that you can tolerate difficult people and situations and not react angrily.

- Use exposure with the relaxation skills and coping statements you learned before.

- To use exposure in imagination, create an imagery scene about a real situation that triggers your anger. Next, mentally rehearse the scene while practicing relaxation and coping statements.

- Verbal barbs are statements other people make that trigger your anger. Create a recording of verbal barbs and listen to it while you practice relaxation skills and new coping statements.

- Use real life exposure to bring the new skills into your real life situations. The goal is to stay calm, cope and not react, and exit gracefully.

Imagery Scene Development Form

Scene 1: Pick a situation in which you typically experience anger. Use a situation associated with a moderate level of anger. A situation that doesn't produce anger would be rated 0 and one that's associated with extreme anger would be rated 100. Choose a situation where your anger is approximately at 50.

My anger situation for scene 1 will be (describe briefly):

_____

_____

Anger Intensity

0......10......20......30......40......50......60......70......80......90......100
none   mild   moderate   strong   extreme

Next, develop a detailed scene on a separate sheet of paper. Pretend that you're writing a mini-movie script. Include details that would normally be part of this situation. Consider the following items:

> other people who were present, the clothes people were wearing, the place (describe it in detail), sights, smells, sounds that were part of the situation, what others said, tone of voice, facial expressions of others, physical sensations you felt, thoughts you had, what you said, and what you did.

Describe how things unfolded from start to finish. Make sure that the scene is written in such a way that you can really imagine yourself as a participant and not just as an observer.

Scene 2: After you've completed the exposure exercises for scene 1, choose another situation where you typically experience anger. This time, use a situation that's usually associated with a stronger level of anger. Repeat the same procedures to develop the second scene.

My anger situation for scene 2 will be (describe briefly):

_____

_____

Anger Intensity

0......10......20......30......40......50......60......70......80......90......100
none   mild   moderate   strong   extreme

Again, develop a detailed scene on a separate page.

[Howard Kassinove, Ph.D., and Raymond Chip Tafrate, Ph.D., *Anger Management: The Complete Treatment Guidebook for Practitioners* © 2002]

CHAPTER 10

EXPRESS YOUR ANGER IN AN ASSERTIVE, PRODUCTIVE WAY

Assertion is vital within a relationship. Aggression is not....

— GEORGIA LANOIL, psychologist

We live in an imperfect world. No matter how good your relationships are with family members, friends, and co-workers, there will be times when you feel annoyed and angry after they act badly. Is it OK to express yourself when others act in ways that are inconsiderate, annoying, and disrespectful?

Perhaps you think expression is *OK*, even required, so that others will know exactly where you stand. So you let it all out — just as you feel it. Unfortunately, others might not like your strong reactions, and you may suffer the loss of family relationships, friendships, jobs, and so forth. Or perhaps you think it's *not OK*, because you don't believe you have the skills to express yourself in difficult situations. You just don't know what to say. You might be concerned that if you do express yourself, the discussion will get heated and turn into an argument.

You've already racked up some life experiences that show you that bad things can happen when you express your anger. Thus, there might be times when you're not honest about how you feel because you've had difficulty controlling your emotional reactions. So you might say nothing and fume silently when people treat you badly. This often leads to built-up resentment. Then, when you do finally express yourself, you might do so in ways that are too strong, aggressive, and ineffective. This is a common pattern for people who struggle with anger — they don't know how to express their feelings in a productive manner or to directly ask for what they want. If these patterns fit you, it's time to learn how to be more assertive when dealing with others.

Assertiveness training was developed in 1970 by psychologists Robert Alberti and Michael Emmons, who wrote *Your Perfect Right.* It is one of the most powerful anger control techniques ever developed by psychologists. Assertiveness skills help you express emotional reactions appropriately, stand up for yourself during conflicts, and negotiate solutions with others in a fair and reasonable way. They also minimize emotional blocks that stand in the way of acting in your own best interests. Learning to act assertively goes hand-in-hand with keeping anger down.

GOALS OF ACTING ASSERTIVELY

When you act assertively, you use appropriate words and behaviors as you try to reduce conflict and find solutions to problems. Notice that we said, "try." We believe that assertive communication gives you the best chance of working things out — but it isn't a guarantee. Let's look at a few examples.

Judith is a forty-two-year-old married executive with two young children. She generally gets along well with her boss, Malaya. Nevertheless, she becomes angry when Malaya schedules out-of-town business trips without telling her in advance. These trips often interfere with her family obligations. Judith usually cancels her family plans in order to meet her boss' expectations. Inside, she feels angry and resentful and is considering finding a new job.

Tom has had a long-standing friendship with Reginald. However, in the past year, Tom has noticed that Reginald often cancels plans at the last minute or is late to lunch appointments. Tom realizes that Reginald is busy with a new job, so he doesn't say anything about the inconsiderate behavior.

Miguel, a twenty-eight-year-old newly married man, was simply "told" by his wife Angie that they would be celebrating New

Year's Eve with her mother. Angie frequently commits the couple to spending time with her family without asking Miguel. He usually goes along. However, the get-togethers with her family don't go well because Miguel often loses his temper over something minor that Angie says or does.

If Judith, Tom, and Miguel assertively approach the people who started their episodes of anger, they might be able to produce a reasonable solution. If Judith expresses her concerns assertively, her boss might listen to them and change the way she schedules her travel. Likewise, if Tom approaches Reginald they might be able to continue their friendship in a way that's satisfying for both of them. And, if Miguel assertively talks to his wife about how they schedule weekend and holiday events and how to appropriately consider her mother's desires, they might work out an agreeable plan.

Nevertheless, we're realistic and understand that assertiveness might not produce the desired result. That's why assertiveness is paired with our other anger control techniques. If assertiveness works and produces less conflict and distress, fantastic! If not, you've already been introduced to other skills to help you reduce anger.

When we teach people to be assertive, we think of both short-term and long-term goals. In the short term, the goal is to find a solution to a particular problem. However, before a solution can be found, there's usually some emotional baggage to overcome. The anger that develops from conflicts, rejections, and unfair treatment stands in the way of clear thinking about potential solutions and interferes with your working together with the other person. That's why assertiveness adds an anger expression step to the social problem solving technique we taught you in chapter 5.

When anger is relatively mild, it's often possible to simply brainstorm with the other person to come up with a solution that will solve the problem. Judith, for example, might be able to work out a solution in which she provides a list of possible travel dates in advance for her boss to choose from. Of course, finding an agreeable solution depends on the situation and the cooperativeness of the other person. An agreement is more likely to be reached if Judith is viewed as a needed and respected employee and Malaya is a reasonable leader. In contrast, if her anger is strong and is expressed inappropriately, or if Malaya is also harboring anger at her for other reasons, then the anger will have to be resolved before solutions are created and accepted.

In assertiveness, there's also a long-term goal: to develop an *automatic* way of approaching difficult situations that involves expressing feelings and developing solutions. As a newly married man, for example, Miguel can expect a lot of life and family conflicts as the years go along. That's only normal. It will be best if he learns to *automatically* respond with an appropriate expression of his annoyance while he communicates his desire to resolve the issue at hand. The more automatic that assertiveness becomes, the more likely it is that Miguel will live a calmer and happier life.

WHEN TO BE ASSERTIVE

It isn't necessary to be assertive in every situation. As we said in chapter 4, not all unpleasant behavior has to be confronted, not all disagreements have to be discussed, and not all problems can be resolved. You have to choose which situations call for assertive reactions and which ones can be let go. Usually when there's an ongoing worthwhile relationship, like those Judith, Tom, and Miguel have, it's worth your time and energy to try to improve the situation through assertive communication.

HOW TO BE ASSERTIVE

The three topics covered in this chapter that will help you become more assertive are the following:

1. understanding the differences among assertive, unassertive, and verbally aggressive responses
2. understanding your rights in conflicts and disappointing situations, while also appreciating the viewpoint and rights of others
3. developing an assertive lifestyle through repeated practice

Let's first look at some definitions and examples of assertive reactions. Then we can compare those reactions to others that are less desirable. When you express your thoughts and feelings assertively, you communicate directly, honestly, and appropriately.

Communicating directly means you meet with, and talk or write to, the person you're having a conflict with. Indirect communications, in contrast, are such things as gossiping, complaining, or having someone else communicate for you. Communicating honestly and appropriately means that when you have feelings, beliefs, desires, opinions, and preferences about others, you express them at the right time, without sarcasm, without screaming, without exaggeration, and without going on and on.

We said that all humans feel annoyed or angry from time to time. Judith felt this way when her boss scheduled business trips without consulting her. Tom felt this way because of Reginald's inconsiderate behavior. And Miguel felt this way when his wife arranged for New Year's Eve at her mother's house. These are some assertive responses they could make:

> **Judith:** Malaya, I felt confused and somewhat annoyed when I discovered you planned a trip for me and didn't first check with me. It was a problem for me. I'd like to talk with you about how we can schedule future trips so they can work out better for both of us.

> **Tom:** Reginald, I felt annoyed when you canceled lunch again at the last minute. It's happened a couple of times and it disrupts my plans for that day. I enjoy our friendship but am concerned about committing my time to future plans. I'd like to talk about it with you so that we can develop a better way of planning our lunches.

> **Miguel:** Angie, I felt annoyed when I found out that we were going to your mother's house on New Year's Eve. I was really surprised you didn't confirm that with me. I'd like to talk a bit about it with you so that in the future we're more on the same page.

In each of these examples, the message given is

- this is what I feel;
- this is the behavior that I didn't like;
- this is what I would like.

These are the essential elements of assertive communication. The basic formula for an assertive statement begins with "I felt annoyed when..." or "When you..., I felt annoyed." Notice what is missing. The words don't convey blame: "You made me so angry." The words don't exaggerate: "I was so furious, and I never wanted to see you again." Also note use of the word "I." Assertive statements usually begin with "I feel..." Using "I" statements makes communications more human, more personal, and more authentic. Remember that the first step is to give a clear message about your feelings to the other person in a way that isn't too strong, so that he or she will be willing to talk to you about it again. The second step is to identify the specific behavior you find to be a problem. In the example of Tom, given above, he could say, "I felt annoyed when you canceled our lunch appointment at the last minute." Notice again that there's no exaggeration, as in, "You can never be counted on," and the words are specific, not vague, as in, "I can't believe you did all that stuff to me!"

The final part of an assertive communication is the expression of what you'd like to see happen. You might propose a solution: "In the future I would like to make our lunch plans on weekends only, so that work obligations won't interfere. What do you think?" It's also useful to invite the person to discuss the issue further, as is done in the three examples given above: "I would like to talk about it with you." Like the other skills discussed in this book, it will take several repetitions for you to become comfortable with this formula. You can practice by completing the prompts in the box. Think of a few times when you felt angry and fill in the three parts of the assertive statement.

Identify an ongoing problem where assertiveness might be beneficial:

_____

_____

Use the three-part formula to form an assertive statement:

I felt _____ (*list emotion: annoyed, uncomfortable, awkward*)

when you _____ (*identify the behavior you did not like*).

I would like _____ (*ask the person to talk about it with you*).

DIFFERENTIATING ASSERTIVE FROM VERBALLY AGGRESSIVE AND UNASSERTIVE RESPONSES

Two alternatives to assertiveness are likely to have bad consequences. The first is "verbal aggression." In this way of responding, your feelings and thoughts are expressed at the expense of others. When you act with verbal aggression, you try to take control of the situation by talking powerfully, dishonestly overplaying your reactions, and neglecting the rights of the other person. The message you give is that your ideas are absolutely correct and the other person is dumb if she or he thinks differently. Here are some verbally aggressive responses that Judith, Tom, and Miguel might make.

> **Judith:** Malaya, you were really inconsiderate when you planned that trip for me. My whole relationship with my daughter was ruined. I'm not going to put up with that kind of treatment in the future.

> **Tom:** I was furious when you canceled our lunch plans last week. I thought you were my friend. What are you going to do to make it up to me?

> **Miguel:** Listen up, Angie. I was enraged when I found out that we were going to your mother's house on New Year's Eve. It ruins the whole holiday. What the hell is wrong with you? I'm not going, and that's that! You'd better be careful about this kind of stuff.

In each of these examples, the message given is "I'm right, and you're wrong," "This is what I want, and I'm not interested in what you want," "We'd better do things my way!" Verbally aggressive responses aren't very effective and can be risky. Judith could put herself at risk for being fired, Tom is likely to produce more awkwardness and tension in his friendship, and Miguel will probably create hostility and distance between himself and his wife. In these situations, the verbally aggressive words convey self-centeredness, blame, and threat: "I'm not going to put up with this," "What are you going to do to make it up to me?" and "You'd better be careful."

Remember, the goal in conflict situations is to open communication. Verbally aggressive communications are likely to shut others down or cause them to defend themselves by getting angry at you.

The opposite extreme is to be unassertive. In this way of responding, you give up your own feelings and desires to please others. You keep your anger in, keep quiet, and avoid conflict. Here are the unassertive reactions for Judith, Tom, and Miguel.

> **Judith:** I had been planning to see my daughter in a school concert, but it's no big deal. I just bought her some ice cream when I returned. There will be plenty of other concerts.
>
> **Tom:** Let's try to reschedule lunch.
>
> **Miguel:** I was hoping to spend New Year's Eve with our friends. But we can go to your mother's. I don't care.

In each of these responses, Judith, Tom, and Miguel neglect their own desires or avoid the problem to please others. Although we all do this once in a while, always being unassertive interferes with building close, honest relationships and can lead to lower self-esteem, tension, and physical disorders, such as stomachaches and sleep problems.

In the long run, both verbal aggressiveness and unassertiveness fail. Neither creates the kind of open communication that leads to successful relations between husbands and wives, parents and children, friends and acquaintances, and co-workers.

BALANCING RIGHTS

Let's now take a look at the next part of becoming assertive: learning how to balance your rights with the rights of others. Being assertive means letting others know what you're feeling, what you don't like, and what you prefer. But what if the other person wants something else? How does assertiveness blend with respecting others? For most situations, you'll have to be thoughtful about the balance between what you want and what the other person wants.

In some situations, rules, policies, or laws exist to regulate behavior. We recently took a very long international flight during which someone had smoked in the lavatory. Since that was a prohibited activity, being a possible fire hazard, and it wasn't clear who was previously in the bathroom, one of us approached the flight attendant and said, "I'm feeling uncomfortable about telling you this, but the bathroom smells like smoke. I'm annoyed that someone has disregarded the rules. I wanted you to know about it." After she checked the bathroom, an announcement was made to the passengers about the nonsmoking policy, and it didn't happen again on that flight.

In another example of behavior that rules are supposed to guide, a supervisor had to confront an employee who was chronically late. The supervisor said, "Len, I'm feeling really awkward about telling you this because your job performance is very good overall. But you keep showing up after 9:00 AM, and the office policy is that the workday begins at 9:00. I need you to conform to the office policy."

Unfortunately, most situations that have led you to become angry are probably based on being treated unfairly, wrongly rejected or neglected, misunderstood, and so on. There's no policy or legal authority in these cases, and you'll have to decide how to act. Hopefully, your decision will be thoughtful. Remember, the goal of acting assertively isn't to win and get your way at all costs. It's to find a *mutually* satisfying solution. This is shown in the stories of Ferdinand and Margaret.

PERSPECTIVE TAKING

Both these stories illustrate the complexities of conflicts. As you can see from the examples of Ferdinand and Margaret, it's useful to develop perspective-taking skills. Here's what we suggest. Take some private time, and think about a conflict you're  having. First, describe the conflict from your perspective. You can describe it to a friend or aloud to yourself (do that in private!). Now, pretend you're the other person. Describe the problem from the beginning from the other person's perspective. We've found that taking another person's perspective can give you some real insight into a conflict. However, if you're not used to thinking this way it will be difficult to consider problems from any viewpoint but your own. Try actually talking aloud as if you were the other person, or writing about the conflict from that other viewpoint.

Ferdinand: The Flexible Plumber

Ferdinand was a thirty-one-year-old plumber who worked for a small, but growing company that served suburban homeowners. Lately, he thought that his employer, who was sending him out on a lot of late-night calls, was taking advantage of him. In fact, during the past two months Ferdinand had fourteen such calls, whereas the other plumber, Max, had only three. Ferdinand, who was angry because he had to spend much more evening time away from his friends and family, approached his boss assertively.

He said, "Armando, I'd like to talk to you. I was really annoyed yesterday. You sent me out on that late call and let Max go home early. This is the fifth time this week that this has happened. If there's an increase in late calls, I'd like to find a better solution so that I don't have to take them all." The response of his boss was surprising. He said, "Well this is a real dilemma. Lately, Max has been having some kind of medical problem where he gets tired easily. He seems unable to work well at night. His doctor doesn't know what it is yet. It might take a while to sort it out."

That left Ferdinand with a decision to make based on balancing his rights, Max's rights, and what was best for the company. Although he wanted a more even distribution of the evening work calls, Ferdinand decided that he could handle the extra workload for another six to eight weeks to help Max and the company. Although what he decided wasn't "fair" to him, Ferdinand thought he did the right thing. After about two months, Max's condition worsened and he took a medical leave. The boss hired two additional plumbers, asked Ferdinand to function as a supervisor, and gave him a raise, all because he showed himself to be an able communicator and was helpful in finding a meaningful solution to an unexpected problem.

DEVELOPING AN ASSERTIVE LIFESTYLE

In this final step, we encourage you to develop an assertive lifestyle through repeated practice in day-to-day situations. Practice and repetition will help you make assertiveness part of your natural way of reacting. Here are some skills to work into your daily activities with others.

Margaret: The Cooperative Teacher

Margaret was a thirty-two-year old experienced elementary school teacher in a small town. That year there were two fourth grade classes, each with twenty-one students. Margaret taught one and Jennifer, a teacher in her third year in that school district, taught the other. As the year went by, the principal gradually transferred five additional children from Jennifer's class into Margaret's class. By February, Margaret was responsible for twenty-six children while Jennifer had only sixteen. Margaret became angrier with each transfer.

Finally, she approached the principal and assertively said, "Mr. Barrone, I've found myself feeling more confused and annoyed each time you transfer another child into my class. I'm trying to do a good job, but I feel overwhelmed. Please tell me what's happening."

His response presented her with a dilemma, "Well, I appreciate what you're saying. But I have to think of what's best for the school. I usually try to make the classes equal, and that's what I did at the beginning of the year. But those five children were having difficulty in Jennifer's class. Their parents asked for them to be transferred into your class, and I agreed to do it." Margaret thought carefully about the situation. What did she want? What were the rights of the principal? How would the children be best served for the remainder of the year?

In the end, Margaret said to the principal, "I understand the difficulty you face, but I feel overwhelmed and have to think about my own goals and ability to do my work well. With so many children in my class, I don't have the time to give each one help with reading. Would it be possible to hire an aide to help me?" In the end, the principal did hire an aide three days per week. Jennifer was terminated at the end of the year, and the principal sent Margaret a thank you letter for her cooperation.

Practice feeling statements. Describe what you're feeling (not thinking) by using statements, such as

- I felt annoyed when...
- I felt awkward when...
- I felt uncomfortable when...

- I felt happy when...
- I felt irritated when...
- I felt good when...

Get used to making these kinds of statements by giving yourself the assignment to do it twice per day for seven days. Don't overdo it or you might come across as self-centered. Notice that as we describe negative events we use the word "annoyed," rather than "angry" or "furious." Although you might have a moderate or strong feeling, in most social conflicts the word "annoyed" will be better received than something stronger.

Express your desires and preferences. Practice talking in ways that express your opinion or desire. You want your message to be personal and clear and to indicate that you're sharing something of importance. Again, don't express your preferences all the time, but do practice once or twice a day. Here are some examples:

- I liked this movie.
- I enjoy the Museum of Science.
- I'd prefer pizza tonight.
- I'd really like it if we could...
- I'd like to go to...on our vacation.
- I hope to see you again.

Describe behaviors and situations precisely and without exaggeration. When talking with others, remember to be specific and accurate, rather than excessive, in your comments. Describe specific behaviors rather than making sweeping generalizations. Here are some examples:

- I didn't like the movie because it dragged on too long.
- I really liked the party because Jackie made a point of introducing me to her friends.
- The amusement park wasn't as much fun as I'd hoped it would be because the lines were too long.
- Jason was really inconsiderate today because he was busy text messaging while I was trying to talk with him.

Accept compliments. When people are complimented, they often reject or dismiss the recognition of their efforts. If this is you, practice accepting compliments. For example, if a co-worker says, "That was a great presentation," don't respond with, "It was no big deal." Instead, say, "Thank you for recognizing my effort. I worked hard on it." Or if your husband says, "That was great, the way you helped Jane with her homework," you can say, "Thanks." But it would be better if you said, "Thanks. I've been trying to spend more time with her, and I appreciate your noticing."

Again, we don't want to turn you into a person with an inflated self-image. Rather, we would like you to recognize that when you're given a compliment, it's useful to accept it fully. By accepting the compliment and thanking the other person for recognizing your talents or efforts, you'll become more aware of your personal skills.

Get comfortable giving compliments. Some people avoid giving positive feedback. This is unfortunate, as psychological research has shown that positive "reinforcement" (that is, giving compliments, praise, and attention when someone behaves in a desired way) is a powerful way to strengthen good behaviors. Get in the habit of complimenting others for actions you like. Become a better observer of what people do well, and let them know. Here are some examples:

- I really liked the way you expressed yourself in the meeting the other day, Dinh. You really captured the difficulties that the sales team is having with this new product.

- Miki, it looks like studying for that math exam really paid off. I watched you reviewing the materials for the past few nights. It looks like your study techniques worked. Great job!

- Hey, Denise, thanks for reaching out the other day to say hello. It always makes my day when I hear from you.

- The new program you wrote really looks great, Brad! Two clients have already told me how much they like it.

- You wrote a really nice report. It was clear and thoughtful. Thanks for putting in so much effort, Maurice.

Using positive feedback strengthens relationships, encourages continued efforts on tasks, and helps you become more in tune with others. With practice, it will also help you become more outgoing — in a good way. Other people will be drawn to you when you use compliments and express your appreciation. Give one compliment a day to someone and notice what happens!

Practice taking the other person's perspective by using reflective statements. When using "reflective statements," you listen carefully to what the other person says and state back the main point. "Reflecting" allows you to better understand and clarify what was communicated. It makes room for the other person to talk because you're focused more on listening than on trying to make your point. When you reflect properly, the other person feels understood.

To begin to develop this skill, form reflections by using the following sentence openers:

> Sounds like you . . .
>
> It seems that you . . .
>
> So you . . .
>
> You're feeling . . .
>
> Here are some examples:

- Sounds like you're feeling really upset about the argument with your boss.
- It seems like you're pretty fed up with this situation.
- So, you're looking forward to getting away from work for a while.
- You're feeling angry that you didn't get the chance to speak with her directly.

When reflecting, don't just parrot back — word for word — what the person just said. Instead, try to understand the meaning behind the communication. For example, if Kevin says, "I'm really pissed off that my ex-wife keeps interfering with my plans to visit the kids," you wouldn't want to just repeat back the same sentence. But, you could say, "Sounds like you really want to see your kids," "Sounds like your ex is doing things that get in the way of you seeing your kids," or "You're feeling pretty angry when you think about her behavior." Try to grab the essence of what the other person is telling you. When you reflect properly, you'll see the other person nod, continue to talk about the topic, or agree with you ("Yes, that's exactly right"). Reflecting shows you truly understand the other person's viewpoint — whether or not you fully agree with it.

There are probably times when the angry outbursts of someone else triggers your anger. Perhaps your wife angrily accuses you of being uncaring. Or, suppose your teenage son angrily states that you don't trust him. Fortunately, this skill of reflecting is useful when you're the target of someone else's anger. Showing that you're listening is one of the best ways to defuse someone's anger at you. Remember, the goal is mutual understanding and finding a solution that works for both of you.

Practice agreeing with others. Often, instead of agreeing with the statements of others, people respond by finding objections or pointing out alternatives. For example, when Tyrone says, "I heard that it might rain this weekend. We won't be able to have the barbeque outside," his wife responds with, "Those forecasts are always wrong. Why are you getting so upset?" Instead, she might say, "You might be right. That would really mess up our plans."

Sometimes, people disagree simply to show their power, flaunt their knowledge, or assert their dominance. Does it really matter if your husband is right about the weather? Most likely, you'll both plan for possible rain no matter what. Just agree.

Practice disagreeing with others. There's an art to disagreeing with others in a way that leads to improved communications. It's a really important skill to develop.

For example, Tricia says, "I think our daughter looks really great in that dress." Her husband replies with, "Yeah, it's OK; but it makes her look fat." A better response would be, "I respect your opinion, but I disagree. I'm concerned that it isn't flattering. What do you think?" Stephanie says to her fiancé, "This restaurant is great. The food is fabulous." Her boyfriend says, "Well, you certainly don't understand much about value. It's really very overpriced for the quality of the food." Instead, he could say, "Actually, you might be surprised to hear this, I disagree. My portion was small and the food seems very expensive. I'm not sure this kind of place fits our budget. What do you think?"

When you give a message of disagreement, others are likely to want to defend their position. Yet, there are often legitimate disagreements, and others can profit from your opinions and ideas. If you can deliver your message respectfully, with a calm and relaxed tone of voice, then you'll both have the best chance for constructive sharing and learning from each other.

Practice agreeing when you're given negative feedback. This is a hard one. No one likes to receive criticism. And when we hear something negative, we tend to deny it or excuse our behavior.

Consider this example. Samantha tells Lucille, "I'd like you to keep this a secret, but I don't know if I can trust you. Last time, you told your husband what I said and he told our neighbors." Lucille replies with, "Are you calling me a liar? I pride myself on being able to keep secrets." Instead, she could say, "I don't like hearing that, but it's possible that I wasn't as careful as I might have been. Thanks for telling me that."

In another example, Vinny tells Ben, "I think you often just use people for your own purposes. I don't even know if you're capable of thinking about others." Ben replies with, "Go to hell!" Instead, he might say, "Wow. I'm surprised to hear you say that. Maybe you're right. Sometimes, I'm self-centered. Thanks for pointing that out to me."

It's important to be able to gracefully accept criticism and to consider whether you want to change your behavior. Denial and excuses rarely lead to self-improvement.

Practice giving negative feedback. Giving negative feedback is even more difficult than giving positive feedback. Negative feedback is best given in a private setting, with a slow, soothing voice, and in a supportive manner.

In this example, Maryellen, a high school teacher, has to give feedback to Lars, a poor student. She might say, "Listen to me, class. Some students didn't do well on this term paper, and it suggests they didn't study much. I'll give out the papers in order of grades." Lars is the final student to receive his paper. A better way to approach this situation is to say, "The grades for the term paper were variable, but generally good. You can get them from me after class in my office." When Lars arrives, Maryellen says, "Lars, I'm sure you wanted to earn a good grade. I'd be happy to show you the specific mistakes you made so you'll do better next time."

ASSERTIVENESS AT HOME AND IN PUBLIC

How you say things can determine how open people will respond to your point of view. Because some readers of this book will be making rules in their workplace or home, we want to note that assertiveness can also apply to written messages.

Imagine, for example, that you're on a committee and asked to choose a sign for the outside of your house of worship. Which of the following would be most offensive to a smoker? Which is easiest to take? Which is neutral?

To most observers, the sign on the left is neutral in tone. It simply states the fact. The middle sign, in contrast, begins with "Thank you." It expresses appreciation, is assertive, and is likely to be the most acceptable. Finally, the sign on the right is threatening and is most likely to lead to resentment for those who smoke. It's the equivalent of verbal aggression, is the strongest in tone, and might lead to resistance.

Now, let's imagine that you're on the local park commission. There have been complaints about dog droppings, and you've been asked to select a sign to erect at the entrance to the park. Look at these three possibilities. Which one would you choose?

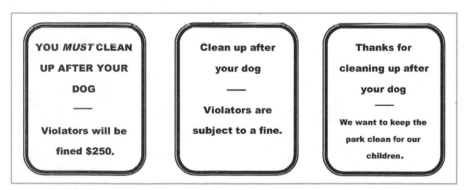

The sign on the left contains a demand ("must") that's likely to create resentment and brings about a sense of mutiny ("Don't tell me what to do"). The middle sign is neutral and just states the facts. The sign on the right contains two important parts. First, by beginning with

"Thanks," dog owners are told that others appreciate their attempts to be clean. Second, saying we want to have a clean park for children is something we can all understand.

A lot of parents have come to us with complaints about their rebellious teenage children. They say that they tell their children what to do, and their children don't listen. Some parents resort to signs on the refrigerator to make family rules clear. Signs and written messages can be constructed in various ways. You can't go wrong by beginning with a "thank you" message.

FINAL THOUGHTS

When you're being assertive, be sure you look at the other person and relax. Use those deep breathing techniques we taught you in chapter 8. Have a pleasant attitude and a firm tone of voice. Be aware of the importance of compromise and remember that your task is to find a solution that lets *both* parties win. *Always* listen to the other person. People, after all, like to know they've been heard.

The suggestions we've given in this chapter about how to develop assertiveness and improve relationships with others involve the development of social skills. These skills add to the satisfying experiences of life. Practice them and observe the reactions you get from others.

Remember, an effective way to begin assertive statements is with the sentence opener "I feel..." That simple beginning is a very powerful way to develop strong bonds with family members, friends, and co-workers. Don't be accusatory; just express your feeling. With practice, you can develop valuable assertiveness skills and reduce conflicts and anger in your everyday life.

KEY POINTS TO REMEMBER

- Being "assertive" means expressing your thoughts and feelings directly, honestly, and appropriately; standing up for what you want; and negotiating mutually desirable solutions with others.

- It isn't necessary to always be assertive. You'll have to decide which situations deserve your time and energy.

- "Verbal aggression" and accusations make situations worse. They shut others down and increase the likelihood that they will get angry at you.

- Unassertiveness means you give up your own desires and avoid problems to please others. A consistent pattern of unassertiveness interferes with creating close, honest, and healthy relationships.

- Considering the other person's perspective is important.

- Being assertive doesn't mean getting your way at all costs. It requires being thoughtful about the balance between what you want and what the other person wants.

- The essential elements of an assertive response are (1) this is what I feel, (2) this is the behavior I didn't like, (3) and, this is what I would like.

PART III

OTHER ISSUES

CHAPTER 11

WHAT IF I STILL GET ANGRY?

For every minute you are angry, you lose sixty seconds of happiness.
— Author unknown

Most folks improve a great deal after applying the seven skills we've presented. However, everyone's life is unique, and it's possible that other skills or types of assistance would better address some problems you're facing. In this chapter, we help you look at where you are in your desire to reduce your anger and what you need to do next.

HAVE YOU MADE IMPROVEMENT?

Now that you've completed most of the chapters in this book, it's time to assess your progress. Consider the four statements listed below, and decide which one best describes how your anger has been since you began using this guidebook.

- My anger is less of a problem.
- I've noticed some improvements in my anger, but I still experience setbacks.
- There's been little or no change in my anger.
- My anger has gotten worse.

MAKING PROGRESS AND MAINTAINING GAINS

If your anger is less of a problem, you've taken some important steps toward improving the quality of your life. However, don't get too confident just yet. Even under the best of circumstances, some lapses are likely to occur as you face unfair situations and difficult people. How you handle occasional setbacks will have a lot to do with whether you continue to improve or slip back into old patterns.

One way to firm up your gains is to be alert to new people or situations that might challenge control of your anger. By thinking ahead and being mindful of using the seven new skills (planned avoidance and escape, social problem solving, coping statements, forgiving, relaxing, exposing yourself to overcome automatic anger, and assertiveness), you can be better prepared to handle difficult situations when they emerge. Beth's situation provides an example of this type of awareness.

Beth: Planning Ahead

Beth was a thirty-seven-year-old highly successful office worker in a textile plant. However, she'd had a significant argument with a co-worker several years earlier that resulted in a great deal of anger and turmoil. Luckily, this man was transferred to another office, and she no longer had to deal with him. The incident had resulted in some loss of confidence and damage to her professional reputation, and Beth had sought counseling to improve her skills to handle business relationships.

One day, she heard that this co-worker would be making a visit to her office as part of an employee-training program that he ran. Upon hearing this news, Beth began to experience negative images and thoughts about the original incident. She immediately realized that this would be a one-time visit, and she didn't think she'd have to deal with him on a continuing basis. Nevertheless, she wanted to handle the upcoming situation with as little drama as possible.

Working in front of a mirror for three days, she imagined the situation and practiced the following coping statement aloud: "I can stand to see him again, and I don't have to respond with anger." While taking a series of deep calming breaths she also imagined several rude things he might say to her such as, "Hope you've grown up since the last time we met" and "I never thought I'd have to deal with *you* again." Beth practiced staying calm and decided that she would begin dealing with him with the following assertive statement: "I feel a little awkward seeing you again, but I've moved on from what happened between us. Hope you're doing well." Her decision to prepare herself allowed Beth to come to work with a positive attitude and with a plan to make the contact as pleasant as possible.

Of course, not all difficulties can be anticipated. If you do have a strong anger episode that leads to bad consequences in a relationship, consider some form of damage control if possible. This might mean trying to repair the relationship by reaching out to the person in a positive way, apologizing, or strengthening other relationships that the incident might have harmed.

For example, twenty-eight-year-old Christopher was involved in an argument with a co-worker that resulted in yelling in front of other employees. After a few days, Christopher decided to reach out and have lunch with the co-worker to see if they could resolve their differences. After the lunch meeting, some of their issues were resolved and they became civil to each other. Christopher also made more of an effort to be upbeat and positive at the office around his other co-workers to show that he was generally easy to get along with. After a few weeks, they regained confidence and were comfortable with him again.

Another way to help you hold on to your improvements in controlling your anger is to work at creating more joy and balance in your life so that struggles and disappointments are less bothersome. This includes cultivating habits like sleeping well, eating well, exercising, managing time effectively, and creating free time to pursue the activities you most enjoy. In the next chapter, we provide more suggestions for leading a fulfilled and happy life.

Setbacks: What Is Realistic?

It's common for people to make improvements but still experience some setbacks. Most people find themselves in this situation once they start to make progress. Even if you've been very successful using our seven proven techniques, it's unlikely that your progress will be steady and consistent. New life challenges will emerge. Some of the skills that you've practiced won't take hold right away, and you might slip back into old patterns. It's important that you have realistic expectations about change.

So what is improvement supposed to look like? The graph on the following page shows expected vs. realistic changes over the course of fifteen weeks. Perhaps you believe that your progress will resemble something like that shown by the "expected" line where you have fewer, and less strong, anger episodes each week. We've found that this isn't realistic for most people struggling to calm their anger. The "realistic" line better reflects the course of progress for most people. It takes into account the ups and downs that are normal and to be expected.

What does this mean? Well, reacting to any single episode of anger can lead you to lose confidence and give up prematurely. Don't judge your overall progress by any single event. Loss of confidence in a program is a concern when trying to change any habit, such as overeating, substance use, overspending, and procrastination. Getting down on yourself for making mistakes or having a setback will only undermine your ability to make future progress. Meaningful improvement means that the frequency, intensity, and destructiveness of your anger episodes are greatly reduced over time. Also, remember that your anger will never go away completely and that never experiencing anger isn't the goal of this program.

If you have an anger episode that's self-defeating, view it as an isolated incident and not an ongoing pattern. Instead of predicting failure, redouble your efforts to go back to the skills that worked best for you. Most people don't successfully calm their anger right away; rather, you're aiming for progress over the long term.

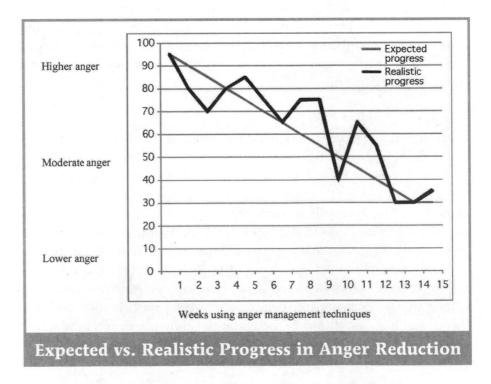

Expected vs. Realistic Progress in Anger Reduction

WHAT IF MY IMPROVEMENT HAS BEEN MINIMAL?

If you haven't noticed significant reductions in the number or intensity of your anger episodes, you might be wondering why this program didn't work for you. Here are the most common reasons.

Not Enough Practice Time

What is your commitment level and how much time have you put into changing your anger patterns? Although you probably read through the chapters, did you do the practice exercises? If so, did you rehearse

them until the new skills became easier and automatic? Practice time is a crucial ingredient for improvement. If you didn't give the program your full effort, we ask you to go back through the chapters again with more emphasis on practice. You might also want to look again at the material in chapter 3, where we asked you to consider how important it is for you to reduce your anger. Do you see your anger as a problem worth changing, or do you secretly still believe that it's everyone else who needs to change? If you strongly believe that other people and world conditions must change for you to live a calmer and happier life, then it's unlikely that you'll put in the effort needed to change yourself.

Too Many Distractions; Too Much Chaos

Perhaps you had difficulty developing and using the seven skills because you're too busy struggling with the daily problems of life. These might include ongoing arguments, parenting issues, health concerns, financial stress, difficulties at work, and dealing with unpleasant neighbors. You might truly want to experience less anger and improve your situation in the long term. However, at this

point you simply might not have the time, energy, and calmness in your life to do much different. If this describes you, you might not be able to properly use this book just now. We recommend that you consider finding a time in the future when things are less hectic. However, keep in mind that conditions will never be perfect.

You might also wish to consider obtaining a higher level of help, more than can be offered by any self-improvement book, to get your life back into balance. Recommendations for finding help are provided later in this chapter.

Overlapping Problems

As we said in chapter 1, it's common for people to struggle with more than one issue. The most common problems that overlap with anger

are substance use, sadness and depression, anxiety, and general instability in emotions and relationships. You might be able to successfully work on your anger even if you struggle with other problems. However, if one of these problems is severe, it can interfere with your ability to learn new anger reduction skills and develop new behavior patterns. If you're interested in reading further about specific issues or related problems, you might be interested in these books.

> *Calming the Family Storm* (2004, Impact Publishers). This self-help book by Gary D. McKay, Ph.D., and Steven A. Maybell, Ph.D., is a practical guidebook for dealing with anger in family relationships.

> *Controlling Your Drinking: Tools to Make Moderation Work for You* (2005, Guilford Press). W. R. Miller, Ph.D., and R. F. Munoz, Ph.D., present their useful program to help deal with excessive alcohol use.

> *Feeling Better, Getting Better, Staying Better* (2001, Impact Publishers). In this book, world famous psychologist Albert Ellis, Ph.D., fully explains his system of thinking better to get better.

> *Your Perfect Right: Assertiveness and Equality in Your Life and Relationships* (2008, Impact Publishers). In this world-class self-help

book, Robert Alberti, Ph.D., and Michael Emmons, Ph.D., help readers develop effective ways to express themselves so they can improve how they react when they're angry. The authors address what to do when assertiveness doesn't work as well as anger expression and how to give and accept criticism.

The Worry Cure: Seven Steps to Stop Worry from Stopping You (2006, Crown Publishing). Psychologist Robert Leahy, Ph.D., presents his program for reducing anxiety.

Master Your Panic and Take Back Your Life: Twelve Treatment Sessions to Conquer Panic, Anxiety, and Agoraphobia (2004, Impact Publishers). Denise Beckfield, Ph.D. guides you, step by step, through twelve self-help sessions accompanied by examples of people who have tried her program.

Overcoming Depression One Step at a Time: The New Behavioral Activation Approach to Getting Your Life Back (2004, New Harbinger Publications). Psychologists Christopher Martell, Ph.D., and Michael Addis, Ph.D., describe their approach to reducing depression.

You Can Beat Depression: A Guide to Prevention and Recovery (2004, Impact Publishers). In this reader-friendly self-help guide, John Preston, Psy.D., presents helpful advice on the prevention of depression, prevention of relapse after treatment, brief therapy interventions, exercise and other nonmedical approaches, the Prozac controversy, and more. It includes a consumer guide to medications.

Sex, Drugs, Gambling, and Chocolate. A Workbook for Overcoming Addictions (2004, Impact Publishers). Thomas Horvath, Ph.D. shows you how to reduce almost any type of addictive behavior, including drinking, sex, eating, and Internet use. Because Dr. Horvath approaches addiction as a bad habit, not a disease, he emphasizes taking responsibility and teaches general principles of addictive behavior change so readers can apply them as often as needed.

If other issues are significant for you, see if you can improve by using one of these books. We ask you to note that it's important to commit to only one program at a time. Trying to follow more than one self-help guidebook is likely to lead to confusion.

GETTING HELP IF THINGS HAVE GOTTEN WORSE

There are times when self-help programs aren't enough, and a higher level of assistance is necessary. Has your anger and the problematic situations in your life gotten worse since you started using this book? If so, it's time to consider seeking additional help to get you onto the right track. We recommend individual meetings with a professional, licensed therapist with experience helping people who struggle with anger problems.

The good news is that research studies have consistently shown that people who participate in treatment make substantial improvement in reducing their anger reactions. There are several organizations with members who tend to be well trained in some of the procedures we've recommended in this book. Consider contacting these groups.

- Academy of Cognitive Therapy: http://academyofct.org. Click on "find a certified cognitive therapist," and type in your state and nearby city.

- Albert Ellis Institute: http://albertellisinstitute.org. Click on "find an REBT therapist," and you can locate practitioners by geographic region.

- American Psychological Association: http://apa.org. Click on the "find a psychologist" link, and type in your state and city information. Or you can call (800) 964-2000 for an operator who will connect you with a referral service for your state psychological association.

- Association for Behavioral and Cognitive Therapies: http://abct.org. Their website has a "find a therapist" link, and you can find practitioners based on geographic areas.

- Motivational Interviewing Network of Trainers: www.motivationalinterviewing.org. Click on the link "mint trainers." Their list is broken down by therapists in each state.

- Universities. Another important source of information for locating practitioners is local universities with doctoral level psychology programs. You can contact the psychology department to see if they have a training clinic. Often, they can refer you to a high-quality therapist in your area.

- And of course, you can get in touch with us in our university settings. Please visit the publisher's website for contact information: www.impactpublishers.com.

Finding the right professional might take time. Since working on your anger is something you do together, feeling comfortable with the therapist is important. You might want to have an interview with one or two therapists to see who you prefer before you commit to working with one person. It's OK to ask direct questions about the therapist's education and training, experience in treating people with anger problems, cost, and scheduling. If your anger has gotten worse, now is the time to get more serious about facing your problems. Help exists. Go find it!

CONCLUSION

What you do next depends on where you find yourself at this point. You might continue to practice and consolidate your seven new skills to reduce your anger even further. You might go back to reread the materials and then put more effort into practice. Maybe it's time to change direction and focus on a different problem. Or you might decide that you'll benefit from the assistance of a professional.

No matter what you decide, excessive and disruptive anger will surely interfere with your ability to live a happy, upbeat, and meaningful life. For this reason, reducing anger is important. But is it enough? Probably not! Therefore, to get the most enjoyment out of life, our final chapter addresses what psychologists know about happiness and living well.

KEY POINTS TO REMEMBER

- If you've been making progress, congratulations! However, it's normal to experience occasional setbacks as new life challenges emerge.

- Keep on the right track by figuring out when problems are likely to occur, repairing relationships when your anger gets the best of you, and practicing those skills you find most useful.

- If you have a serious anger episode, try not to lose confidence and judge your overall progress based on one event. Rather, look for a decline in your anger over time as a true indication of your progress.

- Common reasons for not obtaining the full benefit of this program include not putting in enough practice time, too much chaos and interference with the problems of daily living, and experiencing significant sadness, worry, or substance use.

- At this point, you have a decision to make: Continue to use this book to strengthen your new anger control skills, change direction and focus on a different problem, or seek a higher level of assistance by finding professional help.

- If you're still struggling and suffering, don't give up! Help is out there — go find it!

CHAPTER 12

LIVE A HAPPIER LIFE

What a wonderful life I've had! I only wish I'd realized it sooner.
— SIDONIE-GABRIELLE COLETTE, French novelist

We hope you now understand much more about the causes and the negative effects of continuing to be angry. Although anger has some benefits, it's generally bad for personal relationships and your health. For that reason, we hope that you've tried our seven proven methods to reduce anger and that they've been helpful.

At the same time, less anger doesn't automatically lead to happiness. There's still work to be done to achieve a truly fulfilling life. Fortunately, there's a new science known as "positive psychology." It's the genuine study of happiness. The advice we give in this chapter is based on published research by world-class scientists such as Dr. Edward Diener of the University of Illinois, Dr. David Meyers of Hope College, and Dr. Martin Seligman, who is a past president of the American Psychological Association and now directs the Positive Psychology Center at the University of Pennsylvania.

Positive psychology centers on the scientific and practical pursuit of people performing at their best. The findings from this field go beyond the traditional problem focus of mental health practitioners. Scholars in this field focus on ways to achieve meaning and richness in life. Positive psychology has given us ways to increase happiness and, therefore, it's an important addition to our techniques for the reduction of anger.

POSITIVE PSYCHOLOGY

Positive psychology research has led to three important findings.

1. Happiness is good for you.

Naturally, it feels good when you're happy. Happiness is a mixed feeling made up of a sense of satisfaction with life, contentment, and joy. Generally, we all want this sense of well-being for ourselves and those who are close to us. However, there's something more than just feeling good. Daily happiness goes along with other benefits. These include:

- increased flexibility in thinking and creativity
- increased sociability and better relationships with others
- more social support from acquaintances, friends, and family members
- an optimistic outlook on life
- a greater likelihood of getting (and staying) married
- a greater likelihood of being cooperative with others
- a greater willingness to help others
- more energy
- a willingness to work harder
- greater enjoyment of work
- greater job productivity
- earning more money
- an increased willingness to be charitable
- being better liked by others
- greater resilience in the face of life's hardships
- a stronger immune system and, therefore, better health
- a longer life

If you're a manager, supervisor, or executive, you'll be interested in knowing that happy employees are more likely to show up for work on time, receive better customer evaluations, and take fewer sick days. In terms of your family life, a lot of good things are likely to happen for you and your family members if you increase your sense of happiness and the happiness of your wife or husband and children. Happy family members experience a calmer home life with less conflict and a better quality of life.

We wrote this chapter because we think that working to develop positive feelings is an approach you might have overlooked as you seek to reduce your anger! In fact, a lot of your anger might simply disappear if you do what we recommend below to increase your happiness level. After all, it's hard to be happy and angry at the same time.

2. Living happily doesn't mean you'll never have negative feelings.

To live a truly enriched life, you'll have to experience a range of feelings, *some* of them negative. That's how humans respond. As a reaction to negative life events, milder negative feelings — such as annoyance, regret, concern, and sadness — serve two useful and important functions. First, they provide you with feedback about how your life is going, and, second, they help you recognize when you're happy by providing you with a contrast.

A balanced emotional life is a requirement for mental health. Positive emotions and peace balanced by occasional annoyance and other mild negative emotions is the formula for success. In contrast, strong negative feelings such as anger and rage disrupt happiness.

3. Happiness is achievable.

Positive psychology has shown us that, with some attention and effort, you can increase your happiness level. This increase requires two steps: first, reduce anger and unhappiness and, second, learn how to maximize good feelings.

The good news is that happiness is equally available to you if you're rich or poor, old or young, a woman or a man. Of course, some circumstances lead almost all people to become temporarily unhappy. Two examples are being widowed and having to face a life-threatening illness or disability. Even here, there's great opportunity for daily happiness with straight, rational thinking and decreasing the focus on the unpleasant aspects of life.

You might be surprised to learn, for example, that even after life-altering events such as becoming disabled, people return to their

pre-disability happiness levels after about a year. They learn to adjust, and they derive new sources of happiness. At the other extreme, people who win large amounts of money in lotteries become very happy *for a while*. Then, they also return to their pre-millionaire happiness (or unhappiness) levels. Although tragedy and good fortune can alter happiness, the effects are usually temporary.

That brings up the all-important question. How much of your happiness is due to external factors? In other words, to what extent is your happiness or unhappiness due to your new car,

new home, losing a job, getting an increase in salary, losing some of your vision, buying a new sofa, or buying that new dress or suit? In actuality, not much! According to studies by Dr. Sonja Lyubomirsky, a professor of psychology at the University of California at Riverside, what you have or don't have probably affects only about 10 percent of your happiness. Even in those cases, the happiness caused by a job promotion, buying a new, powerful personal computer, or getting into the school of your choice typically lasts for only a few months.

New work responsibilities quickly offset the joy that comes with the promotion. The powerful new computer is quickly outpaced by more powerful computers. And happiness from getting into that school of your choice is quickly replaced by the grind of attending classes, writing term papers, and taking anxiety-provoking examinations. We're not trying to take away the initial joy that comes from these events; but it's important to put them into perspective. A lot of adults wrongly believe that collecting possessions or pursuing achievements and status can bring happiness. At best, these strategies result in a fleeting sense of well-being.

What else accounts for happiness? Well, a lot comes from your human nature. Some people seem to be naturally happy. In fact, this might account for half of your happiness level. Some folks just seem to be born with a temperament to let negative events have little effect on them. Other people, as the saying goes, "make mountains out of molehills." They take everything to heart. They're offended and feel hurt by the smallest of slights. They react strongly to events that will realistically have little effect on their life. This natural tendency to be relatively happy, or relatively angry or depressed, is a part of all of us.

However, a natural tendency isn't totally unchangeable. Some of us were born with a natural tendency to be tall. Malnutrition wouldn't allow that tendency to be fulfilled. Some of us were born with great talents to be musicians, artists, or mathematicians. To be fulfilled, those talents have to be developed with education, family support, and a lot of hard work. In the same way, natural tendencies to happiness require thoughtful development.

It appears that what you possess, or don't possess, along with your natural tendency accounts for about 60 percent of your happiness level. This means that some 40 percent of happiness comes from other factors, such as your behavioral and social patterns and how you think about your life. Just as you can rethink negative events in your life to improve the way you act when you're angry, you can think about life and your social world in a way that increases your happiness. The well-adjusted person is someone who seeks genuine happiness by mastering her or his thought patterns, arranging the social world to increase joyful moments and lessen unpleasant experiences, and taking an active approach to making life better.

NINE HAPPINESS STEPS

Let's now consider some of the findings from positive psychology and the steps you can take to live a happier, more upbeat life. These ideas and behaviors will help you deal with future anger triggers, so you can easily bounce back from the negative events that we all experience.

Step 1: Begin by thinking about going beyond anger reduction.

Focus on anger reduction as being only the *first part* of your journey to happiness. Make a commitment to take active steps to live a happier life by reminding yourself each day that happiness is a goal worth pursuing. It's easy to get caught up with the obligations, responsibilities, and the problems of life and not put energy toward finding joy. You might even consider telling people you're close to that your priorities have shifted and that experiencing moments of joy is now something that's important to you. Be public about your plans for a new garden, to take an adult education class, or to take a trip in the next six months. Communicate words of hope for the future, as opposed to focusing on past negative events. You deserve more joy. Are you willing to work for it?

Step 2: Recognize and foster your unique set of talents and assets.

You're better at some things, and always will be, than at others. You might be an artist, talented with tools, or great with computers. You

might enjoy and know about cooking more than you do about Shakespeare or history. As much as possible, focus on your interests, talents, and strengths as you move through your daily life. Remember that we're not all equal and almost every skill is to be valued.

Consider the left-handed baseball batter who tries to develop skill as a righty. It will take lots of time and is typically doomed to failure. It's much better for that person to enhance left-handed skills. Think about your natural talents and skills, and put some energy into developing them even further.

Step 3: Understand that increases in good feelings help you do better in difficult situations.

You'll be more likely to successfully use anger reduction techniques based on avoidance and escape, social problem solving, and changing your thinking about problems if you've been happy.

Consider some simple things you can do to become more aware of the good parts of your life. For example, if you're married, develop an agreement with your husband or wife that at breakfast you'll talk only about positive events. Make a list of possibilities. These might include the fact that your child met a new friend, that your bulbs are coming up in the garden, or that you're looking forward to the next episode of a TV series you enjoy. Talk *only* about the positive side of these events.

At work, you might decide that you'll report at least one positive event to a co-worker over morning coffee. There's little sense in just complaining about traffic, the weather, or the difficult parking situation. Focus on the positive as an intentional act on your part. You can also try bringing out the positives in others. For example, you might ask your child, wife, or co-worker, "What's the one best thing that happened to you today (or this week)?" One of our colleagues, Bruce, told us that before going to sleep, he and his fiancée tell each other about something they appreciated that day. Try it!

We're not suggesting you always focus on the positive. There will certainly be plenty of problems and difficulties to deal with. However, by having more balance, you'll be better able to function during negative and challenging moments.

Step 4: Take small steps to increase happiness.

We don't expect that you'll suddenly become joyous if you've been suffering with angry feelings and difficult relationships for years. However, we've observed that angry folks limit their lives in needless ways. They continue to think and talk *only* about negative events, and they limit the range of their activities. Increases in happiness come in small steps. If you've limited your activities, take active steps to behave differently. Go to the mall, to the aquarium, to the movies, to the beach on a summer evening, fishing, for a walk in the park, to the circus, or to a live theater production. Try to do something each day that will create a moment of joy. Do it sooner, rather than later.

Step 5: Embrace humor and silliness.

People who struggle with anger problems spend so much time seeing the negatives in their lives, complaining about their anger triggers, and thinking of how to get even with others that they lose the capacity to be silly and to enjoy life. Is this you? If so, try to slip more humor into your social relationships. If you're a parent, find ways to joke with your children. At work, you might try to be less serious and more fun loving. With your husband or boyfriend, you could be more playful and teasing. Try to laugh more with the people you know and love.

The good news is that humor is all around us. It's easy to rent DVDs of stand-up comics, romantic comedies, and funny TV shows. You can search for clips of your favorite comedians on www.youtube.com. Better yet, go to a comedy club every once in a while. Below is a partial list of comedians from both the past and present. Let yourself go. Be loose. Be witty. Be silly. Laugh, and enjoy life!

• Jason Alexander	• Dave Chappelle	• Alan King
• Ted Alexandro	• Chevy Chase	• Stan Laurel
• Fred Allen	• Stephen Colbert	• Denis Leary
• Gracie Allen	• Myron Cohen	• Jay Leno
• Steve Allen	• Sacha Baron Cohen	• Paul Lynde
• Tim Allen	• Bill Cosby	• Norm Macdonald
• Woody Allen	• Lou Costello	• Bill Maher
• Dan Aykroyd	• Jane Curtin	• Howie Mandel
• Lucille Ball	• Rodney Dangerfield	• Dean Martin
• John Belushi	• Ellen DeGeneres	• Steve Martin
• Richard Belzer	• Dom DeLuise	• Groucho Marx
• Jack Benny	• Jimmy Durante	• Jackie Mason
• Milton Berle	• Jimmy Fallon	• Garrett Morris
• Joey Bishop	• Chris Farley	• Eddie Murphy
• Lewis Black	• Tina Fey	• Bill Murray
• Victor Borge	• W. C. Fields	• Kevin Nealon
• Mel Brooks	• Jeff Foxworthy	• Leslie Nielsen
• Lenny Bruce	• Redd Foxx	• Pat Paulsen
• Carol Burnett	• Al Franken	• Joe Piscopo
• George Burns	• Whoopi Goldberg	• Richard Pryor
• Sid Caesar	• Dick Gregory	• Gilda Radner
• Steve Carell	• Tom Hanks	• Brian Regan
• Drew Carey	• Phil Hartman	• Don Rickles
• Adam Carolla	• Benny Hill	• Joan Rivers
• Jim Carrey	• Bob Hope	• Chris Rock
• Johnny Carson	• Jimmy Kimmel	*(Cont'd.)*

• Will Rogers	• Red Skelton	• Ben Turpin
• Ray Romano	• Yakov Smirnoff	• Christopher Walken
• Rita Rudner	• David Spade	• Jimmie Walker
• Nipsey Russell	• Howard Stern	• Robin Williams
• Adam Sandler	• Jon Stewart	• Flip Wilson
• Peter Sellers	• Ben Stiller	• Jonathan Winters
• Phil Silvers	• Kenan Thompson	• Henny Youngman

Step 6: Cultivate happiness by nurturing your relationships.

It might be possible to live, even live happily, as a hermit. Certainly you don't have to be married to be happy. For most of us, however, happiness and long-term survival are more likely if we cultivate our relationships. This means first fixing the way you act when you're angry when others disappoint or neglect you and then going out of your way to put energy into developing and enhancing your relationships.

Forming social connections has been essential for humans since prehistoric times. For a lot of lower animals, it's easier to hunt, gather food, and protect offspring from predators in pairs or groups. A lot of animals, such as lions and hyenas, are successful only because they work together. Loners are less likely to survive.

For humans, social support from family and friends is also important for living a full life. Caring friends and family members can listen to your problems and provide a comforting ear. Hopefully they'll be nonjudgmental and allow you to be honest as you struggle with your own behaviors and conflicts. By sharing your thoughts and feelings with others and getting feedback, you're more likely to learn and grow. If you were limited to just learning directly from your own experiences and aren't exposed to others' viewpoints, you'd be very handicapped in understanding the world. Human beings are social creatures, and we learn from each other. For this reason, it's important to appreciate and cultivate relationships.

Human connections also provide more concrete things. Others who care about you can drive you to a doctor's office, remind you to take your medication, or help you with household projects. They can provide physical affection, share important experiences, and help you enjoy the passage of time. Because of these types of benefits, social support leads to happiness and to living a longer life.

So if that sounds good, what can you do to enhance and cultivate your personal relationships? As with most other recommendations we've made, you'll have to be thoughtful and plan your actions. You'll have to take steps to increase social activity and strengthen connections. This means making time in your busy life to have quiet dinners with loved ones, go to the movies with your wife, go to the zoo with friends, take a vacation with others whose company you enjoy, take an adult education course with a friend, go to the mall and shop together, and, most important, eat, drink, and talk together.

We know of fathers who have taken karate classes with their children and friends who have taken calligraphy classes together simply to share a fun activity. If you're single, join a dating service or go out with friends. Staying home and feeling sorry for yourself is rarely of much help. Join a group at your church or temple, and participate actively. To do this, you'll have to give up those excuses that you have to do work for your job or school or that you "must" deal with so many other things, such as housework.

Being with your family members and friends will pay you handsome rewards. We're not suggesting you ignore schoolwork, your job, or household responsibilities. Rather, we ask you to not use them as excuses and to cultivate your personal relationships. Your happiness level will quickly increase.

Step 7: Be giving, and engage in random acts of kindness.

Too many angry people are interested in reciprocal kindness, that is, they do good things only if they think it leads to something good for them in return. They see life as a business deal or, at least, one where they can get a tax break. In fact, there's a lot to be gained by just giving to others. Acts of kindness contribute to physical and mental health.

Such actions sometimes lead to a rush of euphoria and then a longer period of calm. This "helper's high," involves the release of endorphins, the body's natural painkillers. Helping or giving to others can increase your sense of self-worth, minimize hostility and depression, increase social contact, and decrease the isolation that contributes to stress, overeating, asthmatic reactions, excessive drinking, and so on. Helping others can enhance emotional resilience during times of stress and can decrease the intensity and the awareness of physical pain.

With these kinds of potential benefits, you might want to consider volunteering in a hospital, for a religious group, at a soup kitchen, at a local library, or at a school. Note that you don't have to know the people you help. That's why it's sometimes referred to as a "random" act of kindness. You might, for example, send a note of appreciation to the local fire station in which you thank the volunteer firefighters for their help to the community. You could send a holiday card to hospital nurses. You might benefit from donating furniture or clothing to the Salvation Army.

You could send a note of thanks to the teachers association at your local elementary school or to the principal for his or her hard work. Yes, even high-level officials and business executives struggle in life and appreciate such recognition. You could give some money to the local shelter for the homeless or for abused women, men, and children. And if it's within your budget, you could contribute to the American Heart Association or set up a scholarship at a school. Try it. The personal benefits you experience might surprise you. Just consider these abbreviated self-reports, which were posted on the web site www.helpothers.org.

—

A Cab Ride I'll Never Forget

Twenty years ago, I drove a cab for a living. One night, I took a fare and when I arrived the building was dark except for a single light in a ground floor window. Under these circumstances, many drivers would just honk once. But I had seen too many impoverished people who depended on taxis as their only means of transportation. So I walked to the door and knocked. "Just a minute," answered a frail, elderly voice.

After a long pause, the door opened. A small woman in her eighties stood before me. She was wearing a print dress and a hat with a veil, like somebody out of a 1940s movie. By her side was a small nylon suitcase. The apartment looked as if no one had lived in it for years. All the furniture was covered with sheets. There were no clocks on the walls and no knick-knacks or utensils on the counters. In the corner was a cardboard box filled with photos. "Would you carry my bag out to the car?" she asked. I took the suitcase to the cab and then returned to assist her. She took my arm and kept thanking me for my kindness. "It's nothing," I told her. "I just try to treat my passengers the way I would want my mother treated."

When we got in the cab, she gave me an address, and then asked, "Could you drive through downtown?" "It's not the shortest way," I answered quickly. "Oh, I don't mind," she said. "I'm in no hurry. I'm on my way to a hospice."

I looked in the rearview mirror. Her eyes were glistening. "I don't have any family left," she continued. "The doctor says I don't have very long." I quietly reached over and shut off the meter. "What route would you like me to take?" I asked. For the next two hours, we drove through the city. She showed me the building where she had once worked as an elevator operator. We drove through the neighborhood where she and her husband had lived when they were newlyweds. She had me pull up in front of a furniture warehouse that had once been a ballroom where she had gone dancing as a girl. As the sun was creasing the horizon, she suddenly said, "I'm tired. Let's go now." We drove in silence to the small convalescent home. Two orderlies came out to the cab as soon as we pulled up. They were solicitous and intent, watching her every move. I opened the trunk and took the small suitcase to the door.

"How much do I owe you?" she asked, reaching into her purse. "Nothing," I said. "You have to make a living," she answered. "Oh, there are other passengers," I responded. Almost without thinking, I gave her a hug. She held onto me tightly. Our hug ended with her remark, "You gave an old woman a little moment of joy. Thank you." Behind me, a door shut. It was the sound of the closing of a life.

I didn't pick up any more passengers. I drove aimlessly lost in thought. For the rest of that day, I could hardly talk. What if that woman had gotten an angry driver or one who was impatient to end his shift? What if I had refused to take the run or had honked once then driven away? On a quick review, I don't think that I have done anything more important in my life.

———

Small Dose of Hope, Thirty Years Ago

When I was in my first year of college, I hit a stretch where every area of my life was a disaster. I felt hopeless and alone and more depressed than I'd known was possible.

One day, I was walking from class across campus to catch my bus home, head down, fighting tears of total despair, when a guy came down the sidewalk toward me. I had never seen him before. Embarrassed at being seen in such an emotional mess, I turned my head away and hoped to hurry past. But he moved until he was directly in front of me, waited until I looked up, and then smiled.

Looking into my eyes, this stranger spoke in a quiet voice, "Whatever is wrong will pass. You're going to be OK. Just hang on." He then smiled again and walked away. I can't explain the impact of that moment, of that man's unexpected kindness and unconditional caring! He gave me the one thing I'd lost completely: hope. I looked for him on campus to thank him but never saw him again.

That was thirty years ago, and I've never forgotten that moment. Over the years, whenever I see someone in distress, I think of that man and try to give a glimmer of hope in the dark wherever I can — carrying groceries for people, sitting with cranky babies in airport lounges while the mother gets up and gets herself food or to a restroom, talking to tired couples at the checkout line, anything.

—

For Grandparents Who Have Everything

My grandparents recently celebrated their seventieth wedding anniversary. They both had asked for only cards and no gifts. They had everything already and just wanted to be with friends and family. Still, everyone wanted to give money or get them something.

I couldn't give money but wanted to do something special to let them know how proud I am of having them as my grandparents. So I went to my aunt and asked her to give me all of the old pictures of them that she could find. Then, with the help of my best friend, I put together a scrapbook filled with lots of fond memories.

When I gave them their scrapbook at the open house, I told them I knew they didn't want gifts, but I hoped that they would accept just this one. As they looked through it, both of them cried and then shared the book with everyone who was at the event. Later, before they left, my grandma gave me a big hug and said, "Thank you for our book. I didn't even remember some of these pictures! If you and Marcie hadn't made us this book, the photos would still be in that old box and, more importantly, I wouldn't have been able to share with everyone here just why I love your grandfather today." It didn't cost us very much at all, just our time. She still shows the book off whenever anyone comes to visit.

—

Yogi On the Go

I struggle with money and don't have a lot of it. Yet, my partner and I decided to take 10 percent of our tips from waiting tables and give it to people in need. We went downtown once a month and brought about a hundred dollars each. We would give this money to people when they asked. If they asked for coffee money, we gave them five or ten dollars, whatever felt right. Even this small gesture often created first a look of surprise and shock and then genuine thanks.

One day, it was very cold and we decided to get on the subway to make our way home. There was a man walking around asking people for money for food. He was almost crying. I was very aware of how people just ignored the man, as if he wasn't talking at all. Do people really believe that these people starve by choice? My partner handed him a twenty-dollar bill. The man sat down on the bench and just stared at it. He started telling us how thankful he was because he had only eaten a hardboiled egg that day and hadn't eaten very much lately at all. My partner then grabbed his final eighty dollars from his pocket and gave it all to the man. The man started to sob. He started going on about how he couldn't take it; it was too much. Yet, we insisted, and he accepted.

Getting out there and actually reaching the people who need it has been a blessing to me. I'm not saying that it's the best way of helping people; but it's one way. I don't have a lot of money — but the money that I do have is hard earned, and the act of giving is humbling. What's more, the love and energy that go into it are transferred to these people when they receive it.

—

Step 8: Express gratitude and appreciation.

A lot of personal benefits occur when you focus on the good parts of life, appreciate what you have, and express gratitude. You can do this privately by keeping a journal in which you write about those things you're thankful for. Or you can do it through prayer and recite those things for which you're grateful. You can also become more appreciative by taking a moment each day to mentally list two or three activities that went well and to think about why. Some people do this exercise at breakfast. Others do it in the evening before they go to bed.

You also can express gratitude directly to others in the form of a letter, email, telephone call, or direct face-to-face conversation. Consider your friends, parents, children, co-workers, teachers, employees, lawn maintenance workers, postal service employees, and so forth. Some of them are *supposed* to do good work because it's their job; nevertheless, they appreciate expressions of gratitude for what they do.

Here are some examples of what you could say:

- (To a friend): Thanks for being in my corner, Mary. I appreciate what you do for me.

- (To a supervisor): Jose, I found it very helpful when you took the time to listen to me the other day. Thank you.

- (To an employee): Jim, it's very helpful when you empty the trash can for me. Even though it's your job, I want to say, "Thank you so much."

- (To a teacher): Mr. Sampson, I wanted to let you know that I still think of what you taught me in high school math. Your caring attitude helped me to become a better student in college.

- (To a postal worker): Thanks for leaving that package under the eaves of the house where it wouldn't get rained on. I appreciate what you did.

- (To students): Thanks for handing those papers in by Friday when they were due. That allowed me to read them over the weekend. You were all very prompt, and I appreciate it.
- (To a volunteer in a hospital): During my hospital stay, your daily visits and encouraging words made it so much easier for me. Thank you.

OK. We know that this might sound sappy to some readers. Nevertheless, you'll be amazed at what these expressions of gratitude can do for you. At one point, one of us went out to meet the sanitation workers who take away the garbage cans. I said, "Thanks so much for the great job you do. My wife and I feel comforted to know that whatever we put out will be taken away promptly. We're thankful you provide this great service for us." It felt really good to say that publicly. You have nothing to lose by expressing gratefulness to others. Give it a try.

Step 9: Be optimistic.

Now, we don't want you to be an unrealistic Pollyanna about life. Certainly, there are lots of realistic negatives for you to deal with. There are job losses, medical illnesses, and discrimination; and friends, relatives, and strangers do sometimes misunderstand you and act inconsiderately toward you. We've already given you skills to deal with these events with a minimum of anger. On the other hand, so many events in life are unpredictable, and we really don't — and can't — know the result in advance. Ask yourself if you're the kind of person who has these types of attitudes:

- It will probably rain when we have that outdoor party next week.
- I probably won't get that promotion.
- I don't think I'll get into that school.
- I won't be able to sell my house quickly.
- My kids are going to wind up in big trouble.

So often, what we think will happen, won't. One of us, for example, was very worried about selling his home during a depressed housing market. Yet, a buyer unexpectedly came along, and the house sold in just one week.

Consider being optimistic about the weather. In spite of those seemingly accurate pronouncements on TV, the truth is that we can't predict with accuracy whether it will rain. Here is one example from "Will It Rain?" a study that was carried out in Kansas City (http://freakonomics.blogs.nytimes.com/2008/04/21/how-valid-are-tv-weather-forecasts). The authors begin by noting that we could just always assume it won't rain, since 86 percent of days are rain free.

They then examined the weather "forecasters" prediction for rain and compared it to whether it actually did rain. The data showed that forecasters got their predictions correct about 85 percent of the time when they were forecasting one day out and about 73 percent of the time when it was seven days out. But if those forecasters always predicted no rain, they would be right 86 percent of the time. So if a viewer was looking for more certainty about rain, the forecasters would have to be better than 86 percent correct. With this reality, why not just be optimistic? Obviously, it would be OK to plan your outdoor party 86 percent of the time — in Kansas City — which are pretty good odds.

It might take you some time and effort to develop a more optimistic outlook. However, over time and with repeated practice, being optimistic will become a habit — like chewing gum or putting on your socks in the morning.

It would be great if you could develop a new habit of being more positive in your day-to-day outlook. The first step is to catch yourself when you're thinking negatively. Then, consider if there's a more positive view that might also fit the situation. Consider how much better these statements are compared to those we gave above:

- It will probably be OK to have that outdoor party next week. If it does rain, we'll make a quick shift in our plans.

- I might get that promotion, and if I do it will be a real step forward. If I don't, I can ask how to improve my performance for the future.

- I might get into that school. If I do, that's great. If I don't, I might wind up getting an even better education elsewhere.

- I might be able to sell my house quickly. If I do, that will be convenient. If not, I'll learn how to cope with the frustration of having to wait a while.

- My kids will probably turn out all right. Even though they're doing poorly now, with effort and some tutoring they'll probably improve.

The future is impossible to predict. One of us used to worry about his son, who was bored in school and was sent home for bad behavior on a few occasions. His third grade experience was particularly bad, as there was lots of friction with the teacher. What happened? Well, the teacher became pregnant in the middle of the year. Her replacement had a totally different response to our child, and he flourished. That son eventually completed both law school and medical school. The consequences of his early educational problems were unpredictable, and being optimistic about the future was the best approach.

Optimists are happier, confident about reaching long-term goals, and more thoughtful about how to cope with difficulty. They have a greater sense of mastery, like themselves better, and have less anxiety and depression. Wouldn't you like to have these qualities?

CONCLUSIONS

Building your capacity to become happy and fulfilled is one of the important objectives of life. In most of this book, we've focused on an analysis of anger and how you can reduce it. In this chapter, we presented some of the findings from positive psychology. We hope that you'll try some of the activities we suggested to create more moments of joy and pleasure. We thank you for spending time with this book and wish you happiness and a fulfilling life.

KEY POINTS TO REMEMBER

- Living with less anger doesn't automatically mean more happiness. Consider anger reduction as an important first step toward living a more joyful life.

- With some attention, you can actually act in ways to increase your happiness.

- Lasting happiness doesn't come from buying lots of things, achieving goals, or reaching high status.

- Some happiness can be attributed to your human nature. Your behavior and social patterns and how you think about your life determine another part of your happiness.

- There's no one right way to improve your happiness. There are a lot of options. Put some energy toward trying some of the ten happiness behaviors we list in this chapter.

- We wish you much joy and happiness — with as little anger as possible!

REFERENCES AND SUGGESTIONS FOR FURTHER READING

Alberti, R. & Emmons, M. (2008). *Your Perfect Right*. Atascadero, CA: Impact Publishers.

Archer, J. (2000). Sex differences in aggression between heterosexual partners: a meta-analytic review. *Psychological Bulletin, 126,* 651–680.

Averill, J. R. (1983). Studies on anger and aggression: implications for theories of emotion. *American Psychologist, 38,* 1145–1160.

Beck, A. T. (1976). *Cognitive Therapy and Emotional Disorders*. New York, NY: International University Press.

Beck, A. T. (1999). *Prisoners of Hate: The Cognitive Basis of Anger, Hostility, and Violence*. New York, NY: Harper Collins.

Benson, H. & Klipper, M. Z. (2000). *The Relaxation Response*. New York, NY: Harper Paperbacks.

Benson, H. & Proctor, W. (1985). *Beyond the Relaxation Response*. New York, NY: Berkley Books.

Brondolo, E., DiGiuseppe, R., & Tafrate, R. (1997). Exposure-based treatment for anger problems: focus on the feeling. *Cognitive and Behavioral Practice, 4,* 75–98.

Cavell, T. & Malcolm, K. T. (editors). (2007). *Anger, Aggression, and Interventions for Interpersonal Violence*. New York, NY: Routledge.

Chang, E. C., D'Zurilla, T. J., Sanna, L. J. (editors). (2004). *Social Problem Solving: Theory, Research, and Training*. Washington, DC: American Psychological Association.

D'Zurilla, T. J. & Goldfried, M. R. (1971). Problem solving and behavior modification. *Journal of Abnormal Psychology, 78,* 107–126.

D'Zurilla, T. J., Nezu, A. M., & Maydeu-Olivares, A. (2002). *Social Problem Solving Inventory-Revised (SPSI-R): Technical Manual*. North Tonawanda, NY: Multi-Health Systems.

Darwin, C. (1998). *The Expression of the Emotions in Man and Animals*. New York, NY: Oxford University Press.

Deffenbacher, J. L., Filetti, L. B., Richards, T. L., Lynch, R. S., & Oetting, E. R. (2003). Characteristics of two groups of angry drivers. *Journal of Counseling Psychology, 50,* 123–132.

Deffenbacher, J. L., Oetting, E. R., Maureen E., & Thwaites, G. A. (1995). Fifteen-month follow-up of social skills and cognitive-relaxation approaches to general anger reduction. *Journal of Counseling Psychology*, 42, 400–405.

DiGiuseppe, R. & Tafrate, R. (2006). *Understanding Anger Disorders*. New York, NY: Oxford University Press.

DiGiuseppe, R. & Tafrate, R. C. (2004). *Anger Disorders Scale*. North Tonawanda, NY: Multi-Health Systems.

Ekman, P. (2007). *Emotions Revealed: Recognizing Faces and Feelings to Improve Communication and Emotional Life*. New York, NY: Holt Paperbacks.

Ellis, A. E. (1994). *Reason and Emotion in Psychotherapy: Revised and Updated*. New York, NY: Carol Publishing.

Ellis, A. E. & Tafrate, R. C. (1997). *How to Control Your Anger Before It Controls You*. Secaucus, NJ: Birch Lane Press.

Enright, R. D. (2001). *Forgiveness Is a Choice: A Step-by-Step Process for Resolving Anger and Restoring Hope*. Washington, D.C.: APA Books.

Frankl, V. E. (1984). *Man's Search for Meaning: An Introduction to Logotherapy*. New York, NY: Simon and Schuster.

Fried, R. (1999). *Breathe Well, Be Well*. New York, NY: John Wiley and Sons.

Grodnitzky, G. R. & Tafrate, R. (2000). Imaginal exposure for anger reduction in adult outpatients: a pilot study. *Journal of Behavior Therapy and Experimental Psychiatry*, 31, 259–279.

Hilgard, E. & Bower, G. (1966). *Theories of Learning*. New York, NY: Appleton Century-Crofts.

Isen, A. M., Rosenzweig, A. S., & Young, M. J. (1991). The influence of positive affect on clinical problem solving. *Medical Decision Making*, 11, 221–227.

Jacobson, E. (1978). *You Must Relax*. New York, NY: McGraw-Hill.

Kabat-Zinn, J. (1994). *Wherever You Go There You Are: Mindfulness Mediation for Everyday Life*. New York, NY: Hyperion.

Kassinove, H. (editor). (1995). *Anger Disorders: Definition, Diagnosis, and Treatment*. Washington, D.C.: Taylor & Francis.

Kassinove, H., Sukhodolsky, D. G., Tsytsarev, S. V., & Solovyova, S. (1997). Self-reported constructions of anger episodes in Russia and America. *Journal of Social Behavior and Personality*, 12, 301–324.

Kassinove, H. & Tafrate, R. (2003). Cognitive behavioral treatment for disruptive anger. In A. Freeman (editor), *Encyclopedia of Cognitive Behavioral Therapy*. New York, NY: Kluwer.

Kassinove, H. & Tafrate, R. (2006). *Anger Management Video Program: An Instructional Guide for Practitioners*. Atascadero, CA: Impact Publishers.

Kassinove, H. & Tafrate, R. (2006). Anger-related disorders: basic issues, models, and diagnostic considerations. In E. L. Feindler (editor), *Anger Related Disorders: A Practitioner's Guide to Comparative Treatments.* New York, NY: Springer Publishing.

Kassinove, H. & Tafrate, R. C. (2002). *Anger Management: The Complete Treatment Guidebook for Practitioners.* Atascadero, CA: Impact Publishers.

Kassinove, H. & Tafrate, R. C. (2006, November). *Master Clinician Presentation on the Treatment of Anger Disorders.* Presented at the annual meeting of the Association for Cognitive and Behavioral Psychotherapies, Chicago, IL.

Lyubomirsky, S. (2008). *The How of Happiness: A Scientific Approach to Getting the Life You Want.* New York, NY: Penguin Press.

Magdol, L., Moffitt, T. E., Caspi, A., Newman, D., Pagan, J., & Silva, P. (1997). Gender differences in partner violence in a birth cohort of 21-year-olds: bridging the gap between clinical and epidemiological approaches. *Journal of Consulting and Clinical Psychology, 65,* 68–78.

Marlatt, G. A. & Gordon, J. R. (editor). (1985). *Relapse Prevention: Maintenance Strategies in the Treatment of Addictive Behaviors.* New York, NY: Guilford Press.

McCullough, M. E., Thoresen, C. E, & Pargament, K. I. (editors). (1999). *Forgiveness Theory, Research, and Practice.* New York, NY: Guilford Press.

Meyers, D. G. & Diener, E. (1995). Who is happy? *Psychological Science, 6,* 10–19.

Miller, W. & Rollnick, S. (2002). *Motivational Interviewing: Preparing People for Change* (2nd ed.). New York, NY: Guilford Press.

Novaco, R. (2007). Anger dysregulation: its assessment and treatment. In T. A. Cavell & K. T. Malcolm (editors), *Anger, Aggression, and Interventions for Interpersonal Violence.* Mahwah, NJ: Lawrence Erlbaum.

Phelps, S. & Austin, N. (2002). *The Assertive Woman.* Atascadero, CA: Impact Publishers.

Plutchik, R. (2003). *Emotions and Life: Perspectives from Psychology, Biology, and Evolution.* Washington: D.C.: American Psychological Association.

Seligman, M. E. P. (2002). *Authentic Happiness: Using the New Positive Psychology to Realize Your Potential for Lasting Fulfillment.* New York, NY: Free Press.

Seligman, M. E. P., Rashid, T., & Parks, A. C. (2006). Positive psychotherapy. *American Psychologist, 61,* 774–788.

Staats, A. W. (1964). *Human Learning: Studies Extending Conditioning Principles to Complex Behavior.* New York, NY: Holt, Rhinehart, and Winston.

Tafrate, R. & Kassinove, H. (1998). Anger control in men: barb exposure with rational, irrational, and irrelevant self-statements. *Journal of Cognitive Psychotherapy, 12,* 187–211.

Tafrate, R. & Kassinove, H. (2002, August). Defining disruptive anger: the anger episode model. In R. DiGiuseppe (chair), *Characteristics and Types of Disturbed Anger: Implications for Treatment.* Symposium conducted at the 110th annual convention of the American Psychological Association, Chicago, IL.

Tafrate, R. & Kassinove, H. (2003). Angry patients: strategies for beginning treatment. In R. L. Leahy (editor), *Roadblocks in Cognitive-Behavioral Therapy: Transforming Challenges into Opportunities for Change.* New York, NY: Guilford Press.

Tafrate, R. C., Kassinove, H., & Dundin, L. (2002). Anger episodes in high and low trait anger community adults. *Journal of Clinical Psychology,* 58, 1573–1590.

Walen, S., DiGiuseppe, R., & Dryden, W. (1992). *A Practitioner's Guide to Rational-Emotive Therapy* (2nd ed.). New York, NY: Oxford University Press.

INDEX

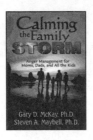

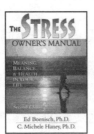
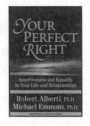

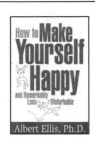